Cambridge Student

D0284100

Shakespeare

As You Like It

Perry Mills

Series Editor: Rex Gibson

CAMBRIDGE
UNIVERSITY PRESS

Inspect
12/17/04

PUBLISHED BY THE PRESS SYNDICATE OF THE UNIVERSITY OF CAMBRIDGE
The Pitt Building, Trumpington Street, Cambridge, United Kingdom

CAMBRIDGE UNIVERSITY PRESS
The Edinburgh Building, Cambridge CB2 2RU, UK
40 West 20th Street, New York, NY 10011–4211, USA
477 Williamstown Road, Port Melbourne, VIC 3207, Australia
Ruiz de Alarcón 13, 28014 Madrid, Spain
Dock House, The Waterfront, Cape Town 8001, South Africa

http://www.cambridge.org

822.33
P3ym

First published 2002

Printed in the United Kingdom at the University Press, Cambridge

Typeface 9.5/12pt Scala   *System* QuarkXPress®

A catalogue record for this book is available from the British Library

ISBN 0 521 00821 2 paperback

Cover image: © Getty Images/PhotoDisc

Contents

Introduction

The title of the play may be Shakespeare's hint as to its meaning. *As You Like It* may be Shakespeare saying to his Elizabethan audiences, 'Here's a play like those other successful plays of mine you've enjoyed recently. This is the mixture as before. Like *A Midsummer Night's Dream* or *The Two Gentlemen of Verona*, this is another comedy about the trials of love, girls dressing up as boys, forests – and a happy ending with multiple marriages! This is how you like it.'

Or perhaps the title is Shakespeare's assurance that the play will be as YOU like it. Whoever you are, whatever your social background and interests, there's something here for you. All kinds of meanings and interpretations are possible, and there's something in it for everyone. If you like spectacle, some violent action, songs, clowns and jokes, disguise, lots of talk about love, and the silliness that people in love get up to, then this is the play for you, this is to your taste.

The title may have also promised Elizabethan audiences that they would find many reminders of their own world in the play. Jaques is the malcontent, the world-weary cynic who was such a familiar figure in Shakespeare's London. His 'seven ages of man' speech lists other recognisable contemporaries: brave soldiers, justices who accepted bribes and so on.

But things are not as they seem in *As You Like It*. Oliver deceives Charles about Orlando. Amiens sings of false friendship. Touchstone and Audrey talk together of feigning in poetry. The seemingly benign Forest of Arden conceals hardships and dangers. Behind its promised peace lurks harshness, cold and danger.

The most obvious way in which the play explores the theme of appearance and reality is through disguise. Celia, a princess, disguises herself as Aliena. Rosalind disguises herself as a youth, the boy Ganymede, and fools the inhabitants of the forest. Most notably, she uses her disguise to trick Orlando into wooing her.

Shakespeare's own audiences would be intrigued by the multiple layering of appearance and reality. They saw a boy, playing a girl, playing a boy, playing a girl asking to be wooed. Today Rosalind is almost always played by a female, but audiences still enjoy the ambiguities that arise from cross-dressing.

Commentary

Act 1 Scene 1

The play opens in an orchard, and the audience is immediately thrust into a tale of family conflict. Orlando, youngest son to the late Sir Roland de Boys, tells Adam, an old family servant, of his misfortune. His father's will instructed the eldest son, Oliver, to educate Orlando and to provide him with the upbringing fitting for a gentleman. However, while the middle son, Jaques, is allowed to study at university, Orlando must stay at home and is treated worse than an animal: 'His horses are bred better'. Oliver denies him both status and education.

Orlando's resentment pours out in a long uninterrupted tirade. Adam is given no opportunity to respond. He listens, as does the audience, to this story of injustice and wasted potential. The choppy, broken, urgent rhythms of Orlando's prose suggest something of the tumult of his feelings. The effect is to give an early indication of his strength and spirit.

The obvious exposition provided by this opening speech can remind the audience from the very beginning that they are watching a piece of fiction, where the conventions of extreme passions, conflict and coincidence are to be expected. Indeed, when Orlando swears he 'will no longer endure it', the expectations of the audience are thoroughly primed.

On cue, Oliver appears and addresses his brother in scornful terms: 'sir', 'boy', 'villain'. Orlando stands up for himself and protests at his being kept in poverty. He echoes Oliver's words with telling alterations:

OLIVER   Now sir, what make you here?
ORLANDO   Nothing: I am not taught to make anything.
OLIVER   What mar you then, sir?
ORLANDO   Marry, sir, I am helping you to mar that which God
      made, a poor unworthy brother of yours, with idleness.

(lines 23–7)

Editors often insert a stage direction as Oliver exclaims, 'What, boy!', indicating that Oliver is the first to offer physical violence to his brother. But there are other dramatic possibilities, and sometimes Orlando is shown as making the first physically aggressive move. Oliver can appear over-confident and foolish; Orlando incapable of controlling himself. However a production decides to stage these moments, the fight reveals something significant of the personality of each brother.

What Shakespeare makes clear is that Orlando seizes Oliver and demands his share of the inheritance. Oliver seems to consent, but his dismissal of Orlando contains a thinly veiled threat: 'I will not long be troubled with you'. He dispatches Adam with contempt: 'Get you with him, you old dog.'

Left alone onstage, Oliver confirms his hatred for his brother. Dramatic convention is that in soliloquy a character reveals his true thoughts, feelings and intentions. Oliver intends harm to Orlando to cure his insolence: 'physic your rankness'. After sending for Charles, a greatly feared wrestler, Oliver has another very brief soliloquy:

'Twill be a good way, and tomorrow the wrestling is.

(line 75)

This single line can create compelling dramatic tension and menace. Oliver implies much more than he says. In performance, his crafty use of understatement through facial expression, tone of voice and careful placing of a pause, can hint strongly that Oliver intends to use the wrestling to rid himself of his troublesome brother.

Charles, champion wrestler to Duke Frederick, brings news from the court. It serves to remind the audience of another pair of quarrelling brothers. The previous ruler, Duke Senior, has been overthrown and banished by his brother, Duke Frederick. The hatred between the two royal brothers is in sharp contrast to the great love which exists between their daughters. Rosalind, daughter to the old Duke, remains in the court with Celia, daughter to the usurping Duke, and they are inseparable friends. Charles tells that the banished Duke has gone into exile in the Forest of Arden and has been joined there by many followers. Charles' description gives a suggestion of the forest's strange and mythical quality:

and there they live like the old Robin Hood of England.
They say many young gentlemen flock to him every day, and
fleet the time carelessly as they did in the golden world.

(lines 93–5)

Charles' words suggest that Arden offers not simply a haven, but an idyll of holiday and freedom. It is like the 'golden world' of classical Greek and Latin mythology, and like Sherwood Forest in Nottinghamshire, traditional home of Robin Hood. You can find more about the Forest of Arden on pages 123–4, but here it can be noted that it is not the countryside around Stratford-upon-Avon, or the Ardennes region of eastern France. Rather, it is a realm of the imagination, a terrain which the audience is invited to explore in the company of the play's characters for the few hours of performance. Shakespeare's choice of Charles the wrestler to give such an eloquent description is perhaps surprising, but the style of speech again reminds the audience of the artificial nature of what they are watching.

Charles tells that Orlando intends to wrestle him tomorrow, and asks Oliver either to dissuade his brother or accept the disgrace that will follow Orlando's certain defeat. True to form, Oliver first slanders his brother:

the stubbornest young fellow of France, full of ambition,
an envious emulator of every man's good parts, a secret and
villainous contriver against me, his natural brother.

(lines 112–14)

Ironically, Oliver's catalogue is actually a self-portrait, and shows that Oliver is fulfilling the role of the conventional villain. Shakespeare provides other untruths in his speech (lines 108–23) to confirm that stereotype: he implies Orlando will fight using 'underhand means'; he speaks 'almost with tears' and 'but brotherly'. Oliver concludes by claiming that if he detailed Orlando's true character, Charles would blush and be astonished.

Oliver's deceit works, and Charles leaves, assuring Oliver that Orlando will be badly beaten. Alone onstage, Oliver reveals his true thoughts and feelings. He expresses his hatred for Orlando, without knowing why he hates him, and provides a glowing character reference:

Yet he's gentle, never schooled and yet learned, full of
noble device, of all sorts enchantingly beloved.

(lines 129–30)

Oliver leaves, determined to put his wicked plan into action. Some
productions stage the episode realistically, as if it were the beginning
of a tragedy. But other productions suggest that Oliver is the
conventional stage villain of fairy tale or pantomime – obvious,
artificial, and theatrically highly entertaining:

this wrestler shall clear all: nothing remains but that I kindle
the boy thither, which now I'll go about.

(lines 133–4)

Act 1 Scene 2

Rosalind is sad, thinking of her banished father. Celia tries to cheer
her, promising she will put right her father's wrong, and eventually
give back everything Duke Frederick has seized from Rosalind's
father. She manages to persuade Rosalind to be merry and the two
women begin to 'devise sports': play games with language. Such
language games were a familiar pastime among court ladies in
Shakespeare's day. One lady would propose a topic, and everyone
would try to outdo the others in witty wordplay on that subject.

Rosalind proposes they talk about falling in love. Celia says love is
only worth joking about, and Rosalind should not love any man,
whether seriously or playfully, in ways that might cause shame. Celia
then proposes her own topic: 'housewife Fortune', who turned a
wheel, sending men and women at random to positions of wealth and
power, or poverty and powerlessness. Rosalind replies that
'the bountiful blind woman' (Fortune was often portrayed as a
blindfolded goddess) is unfair to women. Celia agrees, saying
beautiful women are rarely virtuous, and virtuous women look ugly
('ill-favouredly'). Rosalind challenges Celia, saying that Fortune only
affects things like wealth and power ('gifts of the world'), and that a
person's looks, intelligence and moral qualities are given by nature
('the lineaments of Nature'). Celia uses the entrance of Touchstone to
comment that fools are sent by nature to sharpen witty people's
intelligence.

Touchstone swears by his honour that he has been sent to order Celia to go to her father. Just as the women have just laughed together about love, fortune and nature, Touchstone now jokes about 'honour', and, in Shakespeare's hint of the gender confusion later in the play, wittily tricks the women into swearing by their non-existent beards. Touchstone is Duke Frederick's jester or fool (you can find more about him on pages 74, 121). Noblemen often kept such a character in their household, whose role was to sing, joke and entertain. Fools had licence to criticise the follies of their masters and other high-status people. Like all Shakespeare's clowns, Touchstone loves playing with language, joking to make a serious point. His story of the knight and the pancakes may be a veiled criticism of Duke Frederick's court, implying it lacks honour and is corrupt. However, Celia's sharp retort shows that if a fool's criticism offended his master, punishment is likely to follow:

> Enough! Speak no more of him; you'll be whipped for
> taxation one of these days.   *(lines 66–7)*

The brief exchange that follows about fools being silenced (lines 68–72) may be Shakespeare's comment on an act of censorship in 1599, when Queen Elizabeth's government ordered the burning of satirical pamphlets. Another interpretation is that Shakespeare is satirising City of London officials ('wise men') who persecuted the actors ('fools'). Today, such contemporary allusions are little known, but audiences can still understand and enjoy the general sense: that satirical comment on those in power is healthy and necessary. The arrival of Le Beau provokes the women to another witty exchange:

CELIA   Here comes 'Monsieur the Beau'.
ROSALIND   With his mouth full of news.
CELIA   Which he will put on us as pigeons feed their young.
ROSALIND   Then shall we be news-crammed.
CELIA   All the better: we shall be the more marketable.   *(lines 72–6)*

'Le Beau' is French for 'the beautiful'. He is often played as an over-dressed courtier who puts on airs and graces, using elaborate gestures and speaking with an affected accent (for example, pronouncing 'sport' as 'spot'). Onstage, he usually fails to see that Celia, Rosalind and Touchstone are mocking him. Rosalind and Touchstone use pompously exaggerated language, and Celia uses an image from bricklaying, suggesting that Touchstone is thickly laying on the irony, like a bricklayer slapping on a trowelful of mortar:

> Well said: that was laid on with a trowel.   *(line 83)*

Le Beau's story reveals another aspect of the corruption at Duke Frederick's court. He tells how Charles the wrestler has nearly killed the three sons of an old man. Le Beau calls this 'sport', but the news dismays the women, and Touchstone ironically reveals its cruel nature:

> It is the first time that ever I heard breaking of ribs was
> sport for ladies.   *(lines 108–9)*

The court and the wrestlers enter. Duke Frederick says Orlando insists on fighting, but Charles is certain to win the wrestling match.

This is the first time that Rosalind has set eyes on Orlando, and every production decides whether it will suggest that she has fallen in love at first sight with the young man (Orlando's youthfulness is mentioned repeatedly here). Rosalind and Celia try unsuccessfully to persuade Orlando not to fight, telling him his honour will not be devalued. Realising he is determined, they give him their support.

Productions invariably stage the wrestling to great dramatic effect to show how Orlando manages to defeat the physically superior Charles. In many productions the fight often lasts for several minutes, even though Shakespeare provides little dialogue and only the briefest of stage directions: 'wrestle' and 'Shout' (those in brackets have been added by editors). The whole episode is over in a few lines:

> *[They] wrestle*
> ROSALIND   O excellent young man.
> CELIA   If I had a thunderbolt in mine eye, I can tell who should
>   down.
>   *[Charles is thrown to the ground.] Shout*
> DUKE FREDERICK   No more, no more.
> ORLANDO   Yes, I beseech your grace, I am not yet well breathed.
> DUKE FREDERICK   How dost thou, Charles?

LE BEAU   He cannot speak, my lord.
DUKE FREDERICK   Bear him away.
   [Charles is carried out]   *(lines 167–73)*

Rosalind and Celia offer comfort to Orlando, but he seems unable to reply.

Up to this point in the play, characters have used prose. Now, as Duke Frederick expresses his displeasure at finding Orlando is the son of his old enemy, they speak in verse. Perhaps Shakespeare switches from prose to verse because of the 'serious' nature of the Duke's words (you can find help with prose and verse on pages 82–4). The cause of Duke Frederick's animosity towards the much-respected Sir Roland de Boys is never revealed, but it provides another clue to Frederick's misanthropic nature, and it spurs the developing action.

Rosalind's love for Orlando is transparent in her actions and words. She gives him a chain, hints at a far greater gift (herself?), and is reluctant to leave. In the theatre her line 'He calls us back' often evokes audience laughter because Orlando has not called them back, but Rosalind clearly longs to speak to him again. In performance it is usually evident that Orlando is similarly fascinated by Rosalind, who has struck him speechless:

   What passion hangs these weights upon my tongue?
                                                           (line 209)

Le Beau urges Orlando to leave the court and so avoid Duke Frederick's malice, which is also directed at Rosalind. In his earlier appearance, Le Beau seemed shallow and foppish. Now he seems sincere, and offers good advice to Orlando as a friend. He describes the Duke as 'humorous'. Today, to say someone is 'humorous' means that they are amusing, with a lively sense of humour. But in Shakespeare's day it meant moody, unbalanced, unpredictable. That is because Elizabethans believed that a person's nature was governed by four 'humours' (see pages 72–3). If the humours were not properly balanced, the result was mood swings and extremes of anger, melancholy, bravery or calmness. Duke Frederick's 'humour' is all too evidently that of anger. It bodes ill for Orlando, who leaves one dangerous situation for another which is no less perilous. But his final thought is of love:

Thus must I from the smoke into the smother,
From tyrant duke unto a tyrant brother.
But heavenly Rosalind!   *(lines 239–41)*

Act 1 Scene 3

There are three distinct episodes in Scene 3: Rosalind's downcast
mood; Duke Frederick's anger; the excited planning of the escape to
Arden. In the first, Celia tries to cheer Rosalind, who is lovesick for
Orlando. The contrast with the end of Scene 2 is evident. There,
Orlando left full of elation. Here, Rosalind is disconsolate. Both
moods spring from the same cause: falling in love. When Rosalind
says some of her sadness 'is for my child's father', it shows that
Rosalind is already thinking of Orlando as her husband. In Victorian
times many people thought the line too indecent for a young lady to
say, so it was altered to 'my father's child' (Rosalind herself).

The two women's talk of Rosalind's love for Orlando is cut short by
the entry of Duke Frederick, 'With his eyes full of anger.' He banishes
Rosalind on pain of death. Le Beau had earlier called Frederick
'humorous'. Here his moodiness and malice is seen in the two
'reasons' he gives for banishing Rosalind: he does not trust her, and
she is her father's daughter. Rosalind protests that neither she nor her
father is a traitor. Celia supports her, saying she and Rosalind have
been inseparable friends, like the swans that drew the chariot of the
queen of the gods:

> We still have slept together,
> Rose at an instant, learned, played, eat together,
> And wheresoe'er we went, like Juno's swans,
> Still we went coupled and inseparable.   *(lines 63–6)*

Duke Frederick rebukes Celia, twice calling her a fool. He again
banishes Rosalind with threats of death. Some critics remark that
Frederick's language and behaviour resembles that of Oliver's
jealousy of Orlando, and many have commented that he is one of
many angry fathers in Shakespeare's plays who attempt to exert strict
control over their daughters. Celia rejects her father and takes the
initiative in proposing a plan of escape. She declares that in banishing
Rosalind, her father has banished her too. She says she will share
Rosalind's changed fortune, and swears by heaven that she will leave

the court with Rosalind. In many productions her reply to Rosalind's question is decisively spoken:

ROSALIND   Why, whither shall we go?
CELIA   To seek my uncle in the Forest of Arden.   *(lines 96–7)*

To avoid harassment, Celia proposes to disguise herself as a country girl, 'Aliena'. Rosalind decides to dress as a young man, 'Ganymede'. They plan to take Touchstone with them. Rosalind's plan to disguise herself as Ganymede will result in all kinds of comic ambiguities in the Forest of Arden, for which the two women set out in high spirits: 'To liberty, and not to banishment.' Elizabethan audiences probably recognised things in the escape plan that are not common knowledge today:

- In Greek myth, Ganymede was a beautiful young man. Jupiter (Jove), king of the gods, fell in love with him, and, disguised as an eagle, seized him and carried him off to Mount Olympus to become his cup-bearer (page). 'Ganymede' was also Elizabethan slang for a young male homosexual.
- Aliena is Latin for 'the stranger'. Celia's plan to rub earth or brown colouring ('umber') on her face recalls that in Shakespeare's time court ladies took pride in their pale complexions. They considered suntanned women to be of lower social class (the tan signified they worked in the open air).
- Rosalind's intention to 'have a swashing and a martial outside / As many other mannish cowards have', may be Shakespeare's comment on the many boastful frauds who frequented London taverns. They had a swaggering, warlike appearance and used it as a bluff ('outface') to sell false stories of their courage. The character Parolles in *All's Well That Ends Well* is just such a blustering coward.

Act 1: Critical review

Act 1 seems like the opening of a tragedy. Virtuous characters are threatened by those who are malign. There is violent action: brothers fight; Oliver plots against Orlando's life; Frederick is revealed as a tyrant who has seized his brother's dukedom and as an angry father who calls his daughter a fool. Rosalind is banished on pain of death. But the act contains many features that suggest Shakespeare does not have tragedy in mind, but comedy, with its prospect of a happy ending.

Charles' language helps to set the pastoral mood of the play as he speaks of the Forest of Arden, where the exiles 'fleet the time carelessly as they did in the golden world'. It promises an ideal world of rural happiness. Rosalind and Celia banter together, playing witty word games. Most importantly, Rosalind and Orlando fall head over heels in love at first sight – and love is the subject matter of this comedy.

Shakespeare's skill in dramatic construction is evident as Act 1 introduces some of the many juxtapositions in the play. The opposition of brother against brother shows Oliver's antagonism towards Orlando reflected in Frederick's towards the brother he has usurped. That male hostility contrasts vividly with female friendship, as Celia supports Rosalind in her adversity. The oppressive and threatening atmosphere of Duke Frederick's court is already being contrasted with the happiness and fellowship of Arden. It forecasts the opposition of court versus country that was the traditional theme of the pastoral romance tradition, and which Shakespeare will variously explore as the play unfolds.

The most striking contrast is established as the act ends with Rosalind and Celia planning their disguise for their journey to Arden. Rosalind's gender deception as Ganymede embodies the theme that will characterise the remainder of the play: appearance versus reality. In the forest, things are not as they seem, and Rosalind's disguise as a male will motivate a comedy of mistaken identity.

The mood of near-tragedy that seems to hang over much of the first act seems almost dispelled at the end of Scene 3. The stage is set for comedy and the love adventures in Arden.

Act 2 Scene 1

This is the first scene set in the Forest of Arden, and as pages 123–4 shows, the forest has been represented in all kinds of ways onstage. Duke Senior's first few lines seem to confirm what Celia has only just said: that Arden is a place of content. The Duke tells his fellow exiles that life in the forest is far superior to life at court. But his following words suggest that Arden is far from being a warm and welcoming place. There are strong hints in the Duke's talk of 'the winter's wind', and of 'the penalty of Adam, / The seasons' difference' that it is cold, harsh and threatening. In the Bible, Adam, the first man, was driven out of Eden, a place of perpetual summer, into a world of changing seasons.

Duke Senior claims that the forest's hardships are beneficial ('Sweet are the uses of adversity'), misfortunes are valuable, and good can come out of afflictions. He supports his claim with an image from an old myth: an ugly toad has a precious jewel in its head. He concludes that the forest contains moral lessons everywhere:

> And this our life exempt from public haunt
> Finds tongues in trees, books in the running brooks,
> Sermons in stones, and good in everything.   *(lines 15–17)*

The belief that human beings can learn from nature, that the landscape itself teaches goodness, was common in medieval and Renaissance literature. It was professed to great effect by William Wordsworth and his fellow Romantics 200 years after Shakespeare wrote *As You Like It* (see page 86). In many productions, the Duke speaks with utter conviction, clearly believing what he says. But occasionally a production suggests that the Duke is just cheering himself up, and that neither he nor his courtiers are really enjoying or learning from Arden's adversities. In such productions, Amiens' three-line response is spoken with evident irony:

> I would not change it; happy is your grace
> That can translate the stubbornness of fortune
> Into so quiet and so sweet a style.   *(lines 18–20)*

The Duke suggests he and his men go hunting, but then regrets that the deer – the forest's true citizens – are killed. His comments prompt news that 'The melancholy "Jaques"' has been seen watching a wounded stag. Duke Senior, who has just claimed that nature can teach all kinds of moral lessons about human life, asks what lessons Jaques had drawn from the sight of the stricken animal's plight ('Did he not moralise this spectacle?'). The First Lord lists three of Jaques' similes that criticise society:

- The deer, weeping into a 'needless stream' (already full of water), is like someone who makes a will leaving money to a person who already has plenty.
- The wounded deer, abandoned by the herd, is like a person struck by misfortune who is rejected by society ('part / The flux of company' = divide the stream of friends).
- The sight of a well-fed herd ignoring the wounded deer is like well-off people who ignore a friend who has fallen on hard times.

Jaques then criticises Duke Senior and his Lords, condemning them as usurpers and tyrants who have robbed the deer of their God-given and natural rights to the forest, by hunting and killing them. The Duke, far from being incensed by his critical courtier, looks forward to debating with Jaques. You can find how Jaques is Shakespeare's representation of the Elizabethan 'melancholy man' or malcontent on pages 72–4. Here, it is valuable to note that Shakespeare chooses to prepare for Jaques' entry by way of a long report which presents him in a typical pose of an Elizabethan philosopher, lying full length under a tree beside a stream.

Act 2 Scene 2

Shakespeare ensures that each scene contrasts with or comments on the scene that precedes it. Here, the dramatic juxtapositions with Scene 1 are evident in the setting (the court versus the Forest of Arden); in character (Duke Frederick versus Duke Senior); and in theme (both scenes have hunting as a theme). Duke Frederick thinks some of his servants have helped Rosalind and Celia to flee. Touchstone is reported missing, and Orlando is thought to be with Rosalind and Celia. Frederick orders Orlando or Oliver to be brought to him, and the fugitives to be hunted down (he seems to have forgotten that he banished Rosalind).

Scene 2 is very short, but it is vital to the play. It provides the juxtapositions just noted, insight into character, and information to advance the plot. It is sometimes staged to deepen the impression of Duke Frederick's tyranny, by showing his Lords to be fearful of how he will behave. In one production, his command that Orlando be brought before him ('"Fetch that gallant hither"') was dictated to an obviously terrified scribe.

Act 2 Scene 3

In Scene 2, Duke Frederick was told that Orlando was sure to be with Celia and Rosalind. But Scene 3 shows that Orlando has returned home after the wrestling match (as he said he would at the end of Act 1 Scene 2). Adam greets him with threatening news.

There is a story that Shakespeare himself played Adam at the Globe Theatre. If the story is true, how did he play the faithful old servant? Shakespeare was in his thirties, Adam is almost 80 years old. The answer seems to be that Adam's language, with its repetitions and questions, gives any actor the opportunity to create the impression of an old man, fearful and rambling, his mind sometimes wandering. Adam lists Orlando's virtues ('gentle', 'sweet', etc.), but goes on to tell how such good qualities are hated in the unnatural world of the court:

>   your virtues, gentle master,
> Are sanctified and holy traitors to you.
> O what a world is this when what is comely
> Envenoms him that bears it!   *(lines 12–15)*

Adam reveals that Oliver is plotting to kill Orlando, and urges Orlando to leave. But Orlando prefers to face his murderous brother rather than become a beggar or highwayman (a decision which critics have variously interpreted as showing either his nobility or his snobbery). Adam offers his life savings and service to Orlando, saying that God will look after him. His words about God feeding the ravens and sparrows echo lines from the Bible (Psalms 147.9, Matthew 10.29). Some actors have played Adam's lines for laughs, for example, almost fainting as he speaks 'I am strong and lusty'. But more often he is played with convincing sincerity, making Orlando's praise of the values that Adam represents ring true:

> O good old man, how well in thee appears
> The constant service of the antique world,
> When service sweat for duty not for meed.   *(lines 56–8)*

Orlando's recall of a virtuous 'antique world' and his following criticism of the modern world ('these times') in which people act only out of self-interest expresses the conventional sentiments of pastoral romance, looking back to a golden time. But it has also been interpreted as Shakespeare's veiled criticism of his own times, in particular the self-seeking activities of many of Queen Elizabeth's courtiers. Some critics detect an irony in Orlando following his criticism with his acceptance of Adam's money. In rhyming couplets appropriate to his stereotype, Adam resolves to be Orlando's faithful servant and bids goodbye to his old home, where he has lived for over 60 years:

> From seventeen years till now almost fourscore
> Here lived I, but now live here no more.
> At seventeen years many their fortunes seek,
> But at fourscore it is too late a week;
> Yet fortune cannot recompense me better
> Than to die well and not my master's debtor.   *(lines 71–6)*

Act 2 Scene 4

ROSALIND   Well, this is the Forest of Arden.
TOUCHSTONE   Aye, now am I in Arden, the more fool I!

(lines 11–12)

As the three travellers arrive in Arden, Celia feels exhausted, Touchstone is weary and disillusioned, but Rosalind, playing the male Ganymede, puts on a brave face. They speak in prose, a style appropriate to their everyday feelings, but Shakespeare switches back to verse with the entry of Corin and Silvius, who are stock figures of the pastoral romance tradition that influenced Shakespeare as he wrote *As You Like It* (see page 62). Corin is the wise and contented old father-figure, down-to-earth and practical. Silvius is the young shepherd suffering the pangs of unrequited love.

Silvius' claim that no man's love can equal his is expressed in formal, regularly patterned verse, well-suited to the stereotype he represents. He lists the extremes of behaviour that characterise lovers, each example ending with a rebuke to Corin that becomes a refrain: 'Thou hast not loved.' Silvius' exit, calling 'O Phebe, Phebe, Phebe!', always makes the audience laugh, because it is one of the 'actions most ridiculous' that love makes people do. It is also an example of Shakespeare's mockery of the artificiality of the pastoral romance tradition that will be evident through the rest of the play.

Silvius' expression of love reminds Rosalind of her own passionate feelings for Orlando. But Touchstone, true to his dramatic function as sceptical commentator, tells a tale full of sexual innuendo as he lampoons Silvius' words and Rosalind's feelings. His recall of his absurd behaviour caused by love for a milkmaid, Jane Smile, contrasts starkly with ideal, romantic conceptions of love. He jealously attacked a stone that he thought to be his rival in love; kissed a wooden paddle that Jane used to beat the clothes she washed; kissed the cow's udders that Jane's rough hands had milked; and presented her with pea pods to wear as jewellery. Touchstone's conclusion that lovers do peculiar things ('run into strange capers') echoes Silvius' and Rosalind's thoughts and makes them ridiculous.

Celia's mind is on more practical matters, and she orders Touchstone to ask Corin if he will sell them food. Touchstone, in the stereotypical style of a courtier in the country, assumes an air of superiority towards Corin, calling him 'clown' and claiming to be his better. Rosalind seems embarrassed by Touchstone's condescension, rebukes him, and asks Corin where she may buy food and shelter. This is the first time that Rosalind, disguised as a male, speaks to a stranger, and productions often make it a comic moment by highlighting her evident nervousness as she adopts an exaggerated masculine voice and male gestures.

Corin reveals that Arden has unpleasant aspects. He is poor, his employer is miserly and rarely thinks to do acts of kindness. His words have been taken by some critics to be Shakespeare's veiled criticism of the plight of the rural poor, who had been dispossessed by the enclosures of rapacious Elizabethan landlords (see page 69). Corin tells that his miserly employer's property is for sale. Rosalind and Celia decide to buy the sheep farm and to employ Corin, increasing his wages. The money they have brought with them from the court will now enable them to play at being countryfolk in Arden, and Corin's final four lines intriguingly bring together the commercial realities of Elizabethan England with the fairy-tale world of pastoral romance and its ever-faithful servants:

> If you like upon report
> The soil, the profit, and this kind of life,
> I will your very faithful feeder be,
> And buy it with your gold right suddenly.   *(lines 90–3)*

Act 2 Scene 5

Amiens sings of the pleasure of forest life. His song, 'Under the greenwood tree', contains echoes of the theme of Duke Senior's opening speech at the start of Act 2, imagining the forest as a place where only nature threatens. Jaques calls for more, but is obviously not impressed by either the sentiment of the song or Amiens' voice. He hopes more singing will add to his melancholy, and he cuttingly responds to Amiens' excuse that his voice is ragged and will not please:

> I do not desire you to please me, I do desire you to sing.
>
>   *(line 14)*

The remark is typical of the melancholy Jaques: a cynical commentator who seeks only negative meanings and emotions. You can find more about him on pages 72–4, 121, but in this first appearance Shakespeare provides a vivid impression of his acerbic character. His comparison of himself to a weasel, a small, quarrelsome, sharp-toothed animal, is apt, as is his remark implying that he is interested only in the names of people who owe him money. He criticises politeness as being like the meeting of baboons, and comments sharply on Duke Senior.

After the exiled courtiers sing of the pleasures of leaving court and living simple and carefree lives in the country, Jaques' own song mocks such pleasures, and implies that Duke Senior's followers are fools. He makes up 'ducdame', a nonsense word like a 'Greek invocation' (a meaningless spell – 'It's all Greek to me'), to gather the courtiers into a circle so that he can comment on their foolishness. Jaques leaves with a remark reminiscent of the mordant humour of the television character Blackadder. It implies his pleasure lies in criticising weak and innocent victims (like the first-born children of Egypt who, in the Bible, were killed in a plague inflicted by God):

> I'll go sleep if I can: if I cannot, I'll rail against all the
> first-born of Egypt. *(lines 51–2)*

Act 2 Scene 6

Wandering with Orlando in the forest, Adam fears he is near to death. Orlando comforts him and promises to find food and shelter. This brief scene has dramatic significance in suggesting the harshness of the forest, the compassion of Orlando, and the contrast with the relaxed, sociable attitudes of Amiens and the Lords in the preceding scene, and the Duke in the following scene.

Act 2 Scene 7

Duke Senior is surprised to hear that the melancholy Jaques was 'merry, hearing of a song'. The Duke thinks that Jaques' personality is full of discordant, jarring elements. If he now is merry, in harmony with himself, the cosmos itself will be full of chaotic noise:

> If he, compact of jars, grow musical,
> We shall have shortly discord in the spheres. *(lines 5–6)*

'Discord in the spheres' echoes the old belief that the Earth was at the centre of the universe, surrounded by crystal spheres on which the Sun, Moon and planets orbited. As the spheres moved, they created harmonious music. If Jaques has become happy, it will create chaos in that heavenly order. On cue, Jaques enters, and he seems mightily pleased. Typically, his joy comes from having met someone whom he considers a fellow pessimist. He sees in Touchstone a cynic like himself, who takes a negative view of the world:

> A fool, a fool: I met a fool i'th'forest,
> A motley fool – a miserable world *(lines 12–13)*

In that 'miserable world' growing old and becoming corrupt are inevitable:

> And so, from hour to hour, we ripe and ripe,
> And then, from hour to hour, we rot and rot

(lines 26–7)

Jaques may also be amused at the sexual innuendo in Touchstone's words: in Elizabethan times 'hour to hour' sounded the same as 'whore to whore'. There are other contemporary echoes in Jaques' lines: reminders of sayings or practices that were familiar in Shakespeare's time. For example 'And thereby hangs a tale' was a common saying and joke in Shakespeare's time (it has an obvious sexual meaning). And Jaques' description of Touchstone's wit, 'as dry as the remainder biscuit', recalls that because bread would quickly go stale on long voyages, ships used to carry hard biscuits for sailors to eat. At the end of a voyage, any left-overs (a 'remainder biscuit') would be very dry indeed.

Jaques takes sardonic pleasure in meeting someone who confirms his jaundiced view of the world. He wishes he were a fool, to wear 'motley' and criticise whoever he wishes (motley was the multicoloured patchwork costume of the professional fool or jester). Jaques claims he wants to cleanse the world with his satire, using his criticism like medicine, cleansing and curing the world's wrongs. But the Duke accuses him of hypocrisy, saying Jaques has been a philanderer ('libertine'), full of lust ('the brutish sting'). It would be a sin for Jaques, a sinner, to vomit ('disgorge') his own diseases upon others.

Jaques defends himself, saying his satire is not directed at particular individuals, but at the vice itself, because a vice like pride is as widespread and universal as the sea. He gives two examples, but strangely both instances are of the same folly: low-status people who wear expensive clothes. This seems trivial after the Duke's talk of sin and sexually transmitted disease. The conversation is abruptly ended by Orlando's eruption into the scene with drawn sword. His commands evoke typically deflating responses from Jaques:

ORLANDO   Forbear, and eat no more!
JAQUES   Why, I have eat none yet.
ORLANDO   Nor shalt not, till necessity be served.
JAQUES   Of what kind should this cock come of?   *(lines 88–91)*

Orlando's threats are met with kindly words from the Duke and sceptical disdain from Jaques. Surprised by the Duke's invitation to eat, Orlando explains his menacing behaviour. He asks for pardon for his threatening appearance and makes a gentle plea for help, appealing to the Duke to remember an earlier, better time. His appeal is expressed in formal, repetitive verse, and the Duke replies in the same style, echoing the form and content of Orlando's language as he grants hospitality:

> True is it that we have seen better days,
> And have with holy bell been knolled to church,
> And sat at goodmen's feasts, and wiped our eyes
> Of drops that sacred pity hath engendered:
> And therefore sit you down in gentleness
> And take upon command what help we have   *(lines 120–5)*

Orlando leaves to fetch Adam. The Duke's comment that the world presents many sad scenes inspires Jaques to describe the seven ages of man: 'All the world's a stage'. This famous speech (Shakespeare's version of a commonplace comparison of his own and earlier times) has become a set piece, recited, acted out and quoted in all kinds of contexts. It was often presented in performance as a kind of 'funny turn': an opportunity for the actor to amuse the audience. But many critics have pointed out that its view of life from cradle to grave reflects Jaques' bleak and pessimistic vision: babies cry and vomit, schoolboys hate school, lovers are foolish, writing sad songs or ridiculous poems; soldiers are recklessly brave, seeking only brief fame ('the bubble "reputation"'); judges accept bribes (in Shakespeare's time, a 'capon justice' was a judge who accepted a chicken (capon) as a bribe); older men lack dignity, like the foolish old man of Italian comedy (Pantaloon); and the final picture of old age is cynical and demeaning. That final picture is ironically juxtaposed with the sight of Orlando carrying in the aged, exhausted Adam:

> last scene of all
> That ends this strange eventful history
> Is second childishness and mere oblivion,
> Sans teeth, sans eyes, sans taste, sans everything.

> *(lines 163–6)*

However, some critics claim that the juxtaposition is not an ironic confirmation of Jaques' pessimism, but a denial of it. They argue it demonstrates Orlando's compassion and Duke Senior's generosity as he invites Adam to eat. But the Duke's call for music results in another set piece that seems as pessimistic as Jaques' 'seven ages' speech. Amiens' song tells that nature, though harsh, is not so cruel as human ungratefulness; that most friendship is merely pretence, and most love, foolishness:

> Blow, blow, thou winter wind,
> Thou art not so unkind
> As man's ingratitude;
> . . .
> Freeze, freeze, thou bitter sky,
> Thou dost not bite so nigh
> As benefits forgot;
> Though thou the waters warp,
> Thy sting is not so sharp
> As friend remembered not.   *(lines 174–91)*

The song's bleak picture of nature and human insincerity contrasts ironically with its repeated refrain 'This life is most jolly.' Its outward intention seems to be to celebrate the warmth of the exiles' community in the forest, setting it against the world of the court where 'Most friendship is feigning'. But in performance the exiles' response is often presented as clearly rejecting any idea that their life is 'most jolly'. The 1996 Royal Shakespeare Company production dramatically added to the impression of the forest's hardships. As the Duke spoke his final line, all the characters moved towards Adam, only to find him dead. Everyone stared, frozen in dismay at the sight of Adam's body, and the auditorium lights came up to mark the interval in the performance.

Act 2: Critical review

Act 2 continues Shakespeare's dramatic practice of contrasts and juxtapositions, in which he invites the audience to consider how the scene they are watching contrasts with and comments on other scenes. It opens with Duke Senior, who, like his brother, is also a usurper: Frederick has dispossessed his brother; Duke Senior dispossesses the deer, the rightful inhabitants of the forest.

Other contrasts and comparisons are evident throughout. Scene 1 is set in the forest. It follows a scene set in Duke Frederick's corrupt court, and shows the banished Duke contrasting the goodness of country life with the deceit of the court. In turn, its talk of hunting deer is followed by Scene 2, in which Frederick orders the hunting down of Celia and Rosalind, Orlando and Oliver. Scene 3 echoes that tyranny in Oliver's plot to kill Orlando, but also establishes a striking contrast in Adam's unquestioning loyalty. That contrast is echoed in the final scene, which portrays Duke Senior's hospitality towards the distressed Orlando and Adam.

Shakespeare similarly presents the Forest of Arden as a place of contrasts. Duke Senior's opening speech implies it is benevolent, a place that heals and contains kindly moral lessons. But Act 2 contains many hints that the forest is far from kind and gentle. The Duke speaks of the 'icy fang' of its winter's wind, and Amiens' song in Scene 7 echoes its freezing bitterness even as it claims that such hardships are far more bearable than the cruelties of the social world (in man's ingratitude) and that 'Most friendship is feigning'.

There are contrasts too in the developing love plot of the play. Rosalind and Orlando are now both in Arden, and will soon meet. But Shakespeare's task is to subject romantic love to critical examination, and Scene 4 presents the absurd idealistic love of Silvius for Phebe and Touchstone's mocking sexual bawdry as he tells his tale of Jane Smile.

Touchstone's role as critical commentator is echoed in Jaques' own special brand of sardonic scepticism. His 'seven ages of man' speech presents a pessimistic vision of human life. It is a reminder that in *As You Like It* Shakespeare questions both nature and society: both the forest and the court are far from perfect places.

Act 3 Scene 1

At the end of Act 2, Orlando and Duke Senior, two exiles banished by their brothers, were seen talking peacefully together. Now, in Scene 1, their two wicked brothers appear, with Frederick behaving vindictively towards Oliver and ordering him to capture Orlando dead or alive. The contrast between forest and court life is stark: there is companionship and harmony in Arden, but anger, hatred and murderous intention at court. Some productions underline the cruelty of Duke Frederick's regime. In one staging Oliver was thrown in by the Lords, bleeding and battered. He had obviously been tortured. This is the final court scene in the play (and Frederick's last appearance). From now on all the action takes place in the Forest of Arden.

Act 3 Scene 2

Orlando hangs his love poems to Rosalind on trees, and praises her extravagantly. His action echoes the pastoral tradition of lovers carving their names, or even poems, on trees. Orlando appeals to the 'thrice-crownèd queen of night' to keep watch over Rosalind, who rules his life. In Roman and Greek mythology the 'thrice-crownèd queen' ruled three worlds (the heavens, the earth, the underworld) as Diana (or Artemis), goddess of chastity and hunting; Proserpina (or Persephone or Hecate), goddess of the underworld; and Luna (or Selene), goddess of the moon. The image of Diana is particularly appropriate to the play. It epitomises Rosalind's purity and the hunting in the forest: the exiles hunt the deer; Orlando hunts Rosalind's heart.

Act 3 Scene 3

Scene 3 begins with a debate on one of the major themes of the play: the comparison of country life with court life. But in the dialogue between Touchstone and Corin, Shakespeare mocks the pretentious conversations that often took place among his own contemporaries as he provides a parody of this central feature of the pastoral romance tradition. Touchstone, using clever-sounding language full of symmetrical clauses and antitheses (see page 79), tells that he likes and dislikes country life. He dresses up his empty language by implying it is 'philosophy'. Corin answers him in the same superficial style, telling of the absurdly obvious things he knows:

> the property of rain is to wet and fire to burn;
> that good pasture makes fat sheep; and that a
> great cause of the night is lack of the sun   *(lines 12–14)*

Touchstone mocks Corin's replies, calling him 'a natural philosopher' (which could mean a foolish thinker), and 'an ill-roasted egg, all on one side' (half-baked). He claims Corin is damned for not having been at court, and so not having acquired good manners. Corin denies the charge, claiming that it would be foolish to adopt court manners in the country. To kiss hands would be inappropriate, because shepherds' hands are greasy with handling the fleeces of sheep, and are also stained with tar (used to heal wounds on sheep). Touchstone rejects Corin's argument, insulting him as 'shallow'. But Touchstone's rejection is itself a criticism of court manners, because in pointing out that courtiers' hands are perfumed, he also tells that the perfume comes from civet, which is the secretion ('flux') from the anal gland of a wildcat. Some critics detect Shakespeare's own mocking voice here, and his approval of country moderation and tolerance in Corin's contentment with his life:

> Sir, I am a true labourer: I earn that I eat, get that I wear,
> owe no man hate, envy no man's happiness, glad of other
> men's good, content with my harm; and the greatest of my
> pride is to see my ewes graze and my lambs suck.
>
> *(lines 53–6)*

Touchstone remains cynical. He criticises breeding sheep as a sin, and calls Corin a pimp ('bawd') who brings together a young female sheep and a randy ('cuckoldly') old ram. Each new production decides whether to portray one character getting the better of the other in this episode. Touchstone condescends throughout, assuming the superiority of the court (and himself), but Corin is often played as imperturbable, and more than holding his own.

Rosalind's arrival cuts off any further debate. She is reading Orlando's poem in praise of her beauty. Touchstone criticises Orlando's rhyming couplets as having the jogging, jerky rhythm of a procession of women riding to market ('the right butter-women's rack to market'). He makes up a parody in the same simple rhythm. But where Orlando's love poem is idealised and spiritual, Touchstone's is full of sexual innuendo, all about the physical aspects of love. Once again critics have detected Shakespeare burlesquing the tradition of courtly love, this time in the jig-jog doggerel of both Orlando's and Touchstone's poems.

Rosalind laughs off Touchstone's criticism, but her pun on 'medlar' (a fruit best eaten when rotten) and 'meddler' (an interfering busybody) is also a sexual joke, because 'medlar' was Elizabethan slang for a prostitute and 'meddle' implied fornication. Celia enters, reading another of Orlando's poems, which says he will people the forest with proclamations on every tree, containing wise maxims about society. Some will tell how human life is as short as the distance enclosed by a handspan. Others will tell of broken promises ('violated vows') between friends. Both sentiments echo earlier moments in the play: Touchstone's mock lament on time (Act 2 Scene 7, lines 20–8) and Amiens' song about man's ingratitude (Act 2 Scene 7, lines 174–97).

But Orlando's poem is mainly about how Rosalind embodies all beauty and grace. His praise of her claims she embodies the virtuous qualities of famous women in Greek and Roman mythology or history:

> Helen's cheek but not her heart,
> Cleopatra's majesty,
> Atalanta's better part,
> Sad Lucretia's modesty. *(lines 120–3)*

Orlando's brief description of each woman testifies to how familiar many Elizabethans were with such literature. Today most audience members need some explanation to make clear just what Orlando is claiming for Rosalind: Helen of Troy's beauty but not her unfaithfulness; Cleopatra's nobility as Queen of Egypt; Atalanta's speed (in Greek myth this beautiful but cruel and greedy huntress was given the gift of speed. She vowed that any suitor who could not outrun her would be executed); Lucretia's faithfulness (in Roman mythology she killed herself to prove her honesty and devotion to her husband). Such comparisons are commonplace in the genre of romance (see page 62), but Rosalind's reaction deflates their pretentiousness as she dismisses the whole poem as a boring sermon:

> O most gentle Jupiter, what tedious homily of love
> have you wearied your parishioners withal, and
> never cried, 'Have patience, good people!'   *(lines 130–2)*

Touchstone and Corin leave, and Rosalind and Celia joke together about the lack of skill in the poems. Their dialogue is full of high spirits, teasing and excitement. Rosalind begs to be told the poet's name. Her tone is pleading, breathless and self-tormenting, but it may be all a pretence. It could be that she knows very well that Orlando wrote the poems, but she pretends ignorance in order to enjoy the pleasure of having Celia tease her about him. Celia expresses amazement that Rosalind cannot guess who has written the verses:

> O wonderful, wonderful, and most wonderful wonderful,
> and yet again wonderful, and after that out of all hooping.
> *(lines 160–1)*

Rosalind continues to plead passionately to know the poet's name, declaring that she may be dressed like a man, but she has a woman's feelings. Celia laughingly twists Rosalind's wine-bottle imagery to suggest that Rosalind wants a sexual relationship with Orlando ('So you may put a man in your belly' – a line usually cut in Victorian productions), but finally reveals that Orlando wrote the poems. Rosalind's first thought is of her man's disguise, and she bombards Celia with a multitude of eager questions:

> Alas the day, what shall I do with my doublet and hose? What
> did he when thou saw'st him? What said he? How looked he?
> Wherein went he? What makes he here? Did he ask for me?
> Where remains he? How parted he with thee? And when shalt
> thou see him again? Answer me in one word.
> *(lines 184–8)*

Celia's reply is she would need the mouth of Gargantua (a giant) to do so. Even when she does embark on her story, Rosalind keeps interrupting, but excuses herself with a line that has irritated some feminists but invariably gets a great laugh in the theatre:

> Do you not know I am a woman? When I think, I must speak.
> *(lines 209–10)*

Jaques and Orlando enter and engage in a verbal fencing match, with Jaques criticising love. Here Shakespeare follows the conventions of courtly romance, which often presented an encounter between two stock characters: the young lover and the older cynic. Each man tries to score points off the other in politely phrased but insulting language (see page 67 for an explanation of how the insults reflect common knowledge of Elizabethans). Orlando refuses to join Jaques in rebuking the world, and the two men part, mocking each other as the stereotypes of romance literature: 'Signor Love', 'Monsieur Melancholy'.

Rosalind, using her disguise as a young man, seizes the opportunity to speak to Orlando 'like a saucy lackey' (cheeky servant). She catches Orlando's interest by saying the sighing and groaning of a true lover would tell the time as well as a clock. She describes how time travels at different speeds for different people:

- the young woman for whom time 'trots hard' (lengthily and uncomfortably) between her engagement and her wedding day
- the uneducated priest and the rich man for whom 'time ambles' because both have an easy life. The priest is not tired by study, and the rich man is not oppressed by poverty
- the condemned criminal for whom 'time gallops' as he awaits execution
- the lawyers on holiday between court sessions ('term and term'), for whom time stands still

Orlando is clearly intrigued by this 'pretty youth', expressing surprise at 'his' refined accent. Rosalind replies she was taught to speak by 'an old religious uncle', who also taught her the folly of love. She accuses Orlando of not looking like a man in love, and lists eight signs by which a man in love can be recognised (a sunken cheek, dark circles around the eyes, and so on). All are the marks of someone who does not give a thought to their appearance. Her list is one of many such catalogues in Shakespeare's plays: he well knew the rhetorical power of lists, and used them frequently (see page 81). About eight years before *As You Like It* he had written a similar ten-item list of the marks of love in *The Two Gentlemen of Verona*.

Orlando says that he wishes he could make Ganymede believe that he is in love, but Rosalind scorns love as a madness that deserves harsh punishment similar to that which Elizabethans meted out to madmen (see page 67). She tells how, as Ganymede, she once cured a fevered lover by pretending to be his love and behaving capriciously. She lists at least 17 moods or actions that she used in her 'cure'. This drove the lover insane, and he became a monk.

Orlando at first refuses to undergo such a cure, but almost immediately changes his mind and agrees to come daily to Ganymede and woo 'him' as Rosalind. Some productions make his agreement a light-hearted affair, implying he agrees merely for fun. Others charge the moment with erotic tension, implying that Orlando feels sexually attracted to this fascinating youth. Shakespeare gives Celia no lines to show how she reacts to Rosalind's teasing of Orlando, but in many modern productions she shows clear signs of disapproval, conveying a sense of growing distance between the two women. The final lines of the scene confirm the love-deception, and give each character the opportunity to leave showing very different emotions:

ROSALIND   Will you go?
ORLANDO   With all my heart, good youth.
ROSALIND   Nay, you must call me 'Rosalind'. – Come,
             sister, will you go?   (lines 354–7)

Act 3 Scene 4

After the sophistication of Scene 3, Shakespeare now presents an earthy lampoon of love. Audrey the goatherd is quite unlike Rosalind, and many productions present her as simple-minded, dressed in old, tattered clothes, her face begrimed with dirt, and speaking in a rustic accent.

Touchstone's literary and sexual jokes are lost on her, and he says that her lack of response is like paying a huge bill for poor accommodation ('it strikes a man more dead than a great reckoning in a little room'). This may be a reference to the death of Shakespeare's contemporary, the playwright Christopher Marlowe, who was killed in 1593 in a tavern room, maybe quarrelling over a bill (see page 65).

Touchstone reflects that lovers and poets are both given to deception. Shakespeare's ever-present alertness to such 'feigning' is evident not only in Touchstone's condemnation of 'the truest poetry' as the most false, but also in his declaration that he intends to marry Audrey. Touchstone's long reflection on 'horns' much appealed to

Elizabethan audiences, who enjoyed such jokes: horns were the sign of a deceived husband. Touchstone implies all women are unfaithful, but argues it is better to be a married man than a bachelor.

Touchstone greets Sir Oliver Martext, a disreputable and badly educated priest of a type familiar to Shakespeare's contemporaries (see page 66). Jaques, who has been watching all the while, steps forward and offers to give away Audrey in the marriage ceremony. Touchstone addresses him as 'Monsieur What-Ye-Call't', an in-joke based on Jaques' name being pronounced 'jakes', Elizabethan slang for lavatory (see page 66). Jaques warns against Sir Oliver, but Touchstone sees advantages in being married by a bad priest because it will make it easier for him to leave his wife later. But he agrees to abandon the marriage for now. His song mocks Sir Oliver, who claims he is not put off by such foolery. Touchstone often accompanies his song (sometimes also sung by Audrey) with a dance around Sir Oliver. In one production the priest fell into a pool as a result of Touchstone's 'fantastical' tricks.

Act 3 Scene 5

ROSALIND   Never talk to me; I will weep.
CELIA   Do, I prithee; but yet have the grace to consider that tears
        do not become a man.
ROSALIND   But have I not cause to weep?
CELIA   As good cause as one would desire: therefore weep.

                                                        (lines 1–5)

In earlier scenes it was Rosalind who mocked the foolishness of love. Now it is Celia's turn. Because the two are alone, Rosalind drops her disguise as Ganymede and gives way to her feelings. She is close to tears, downcast because Orlando has not appeared. Celia refuses to take her seriously, and mocks her moodiness by exaggeratedly agreeing with whatever Rosalind says, even comparing Orlando with Judas, the disciple who betrayed Jesus with a kiss. Celia doubts whether Orlando is truly in love. Her sharp retort to Rosalind's assurance of Orlando's love evokes audience laughter:

ROSALIND   You have heard him swear downright he was.
CELIA   'Was' is not 'is'

                                                       (lines 25-6)

Rosalind's tale of how she met her father, and his failure to recognise her, is Shakespeare's additional proof of the effectiveness of her disguise as Ganymede. But she dismisses further thought of her father (even though she had come to the forest to seek him) to think only of Orlando. Her words provoke more unflattering descriptions of Orlando by Celia, who depicts him variously as hollow, a cheating bartender, and a weak, cowardly knight. Further conversation is prevented by the arrival of Corin, who invites them to watch the devoted shepherd Silvius attempting to woo the disdainful Phebe. The switch to verse here prepares for the next scene's portrayal of these two archetypal characters of pastoral romance. Rosalind's final rhyming couplet, as she promises to take part in their drama, displays the artificiality appropriate to that fairy-tale world:

> Bring us to this sight and you shall say
> I'll prove a busy actor in their play. *(lines 49–50)*

Act 3 Scene 6

Shakespeare now presents a third pair of lovers to contrast with the others in Act 3. Silvius is the lovelorn shepherd sighing vainly to his cruel mistress, the shepherdess Phebe, who scorns his love. They are Shakespeare's versions of two stock figures in the pastoral romance tradition, still very popular in his time (see page 62). They speak elaborate verse, the traditional style of high-status characters, but which here is the expected style of romantic figures.

Silvius begs Phebe to show him some kindness: even the executioner, before he strikes the fatal blow, begs the condemned man for forgiveness. Phebe mocks the notion that her look might kill him. Shakespeare gives her a long speech that makes fun of the convention of literary romance that an angry glance from a lover can kill. Phebe heaps ridicule on Silvius for his belief, and in performance often evokes laughter as she glares melodramatically, saying 'Now I do frown on thee with all my heart'.

Silvius' warning that Phebe might one day feel the pangs of love when she is struck by Cupid's darts proves almost instantly prophetic. Rosalind, who has been watching, rebukes Phebe for having no pity for Silvius. She gives Phebe a dose of her own medicine, pouring scorn on her upbringing and her beauty, and urging her to marry whilst she has the chance:

Sell when you can: you are not for all markets.   *(line 60)*

But Rosalind's intervention into the lovers' quarrel has an unexpected outcome: Phebe falls instantly in love with her, thinking her to be an attractive boy, Ganymede! In Shakespeare's time the sexual ambiguity was heightened in performance. The audience saw a boy actor, playing a girl (Phebe), falling in love with a boy (Ganymede), who is a girl (Rosalind), played by a boy actor.

Rosalind has indeed proved 'a busy actor' in the play between Silvius and Phebe, just as she had promised – but with a disconcerting result. As she forbids Phebe to fall in love with her, Rosalind acknowledges her disguise as Ganymede 'For I am falser than vows made in wine'. But Phebe now has only one thing in mind: her love for Ganymede. Her first thought is often taken to be yet another reference to the playwright Christopher Marlowe. She calls him 'Dead shepherd' and says that she now finds his wise saying ('saw') very true indeed ('of might'):

> Dead shepherd, now I find thy saw of might:
> 'Who ever loved that loved not at first sight?'
>
> *(lines 80–1)*

Phebe's quotation echoes a line from Marlowe's poem *Hero and Leander*, and it expresses a key notion of the pastoral romance tradition: love at first sight. Phebe now proposes to use Silvius as a go-between, and he is grateful for any attention from Phebe, seeing himself happy like a poor peasant who scavenges the harvest field after it has been mowed:

> So holy and so perfect is my love,
> And I in such a poverty of grace
> That I shall think it a most plenteous crop
> To glean the broken ears after the man
> That the main harvest reaps. Loose now and then
> A scattered smile, and that I'll live upon.   *(lines 98–103)*

Phebe's detailed description of Ganymede shows how much she loves him. But she denies that she does, and says she will write a taunting letter that Silvius will deliver. Her speech (lines 108–34) expressing her emotional turmoil about Ganymede displays many of Shakespeare's characteristic language techniques (see pages 76–85):

- Antithesis: setting the word against the word. The speech is a series of oppositions: she says something, then contradicts it ('Think not I love him, though I ask for him'; 'pretty' / 'not very pretty', and so on).
- Monosyllables: a long succession of monosyllables helps the actor to speak each word sharply and emphatically. Shakespeare gives Phebe long stretches of language full of such single-sound words. When she complains 'He said mine eyes were black, and my hair black,' each monosyllabic word adds strikingly to her sense of injury.
- Lists: piling up item on item to intensify meaning and dramatic effect. The speech is a long catalogue of how Phebe has 'marked him / In parcels' (noted Ganymede feature by feature).
- Repetition: the swinging rhythm of the speech is one kind of repetition. Shakespeare adds other subtle repetitions of words and phrases, for example the often repeated 'yet' increases emotional intensity, and the frequent 'he' and 'his' express her obsession with Ganymede.

Phebe ends thinking of the taunting letter she will send to Ganymede, paying 'him' back in the same way as he taunted her. But Act 4 will show that her letter turns out to be very different from how she describes it:

> I'll write it straight:
> The matter's in my head, and in my heart;
> I will be bitter with him and passing short. *(lines 135–7)*

Act 3: Critical review

Act 3 begins with a brief court scene in which Frederick orders Oliver to find Orlando. When Oliver protests that he never loved his brother, Duke Frederick's 'More villain thou' is heavily ironic, and self-condemning because it precisely describes himself: he is full of malice towards his brother, Duke Senior.

Scene 1 is the final court scene of the play. But Shakespeare keeps the court very much in the audience's mind as, in different ways, the play continues to explore the contrast between court and country, sophistication versus simplicity. The most obvious example is Scene 3's dialogue between Corin and Touchstone, in which both characters' claims can be seen as Shakespeare's mockery of the arguments conventionally advanced in contemporary debates.

But the major preoccupation of Act 3 is love. In Scene 2 Orlando's doggerel verses in praise of Rosalind are Shakespeare's parody of such love poems in the pastoral romance tradition. That ridicule is made evident in Touchstone's imitation, with its strongly sexual implications. Shakespeare pokes further fun at romantic love in Scene 4, where Audrey's earthiness and Touchstone's wit and sexual desire also lampoon the country versus court debate.

There is more mockery of romance as Rosalind tells of all the actions of a lover that the tradition rarely mentions: the moodiness, sudden swings of emotion and behaviour, whims and fancies and so on. Ironically, throughout Act 3, Rosalind's love for Orlando causes her to display similar violent mood swings.

Shakespeare's exploration of love is deepened with the appearance of Silvius and Phebe in Scene 6. He is 'the shepherd that complained of love' and she 'the proud disdainful shepherdess'. Both lovers are stereotypes straight from the world of pastoral romance that Shakespeare teasingly caricatures. The tradition is sent up even more as Phebe falls for Rosalind, disguised as the youth Ganymede.

That disguise has been the source of another comic event in the act: Rosalind's tricking Orlando into wooing her as Ganymede. The gender confusion gains delicious appeal as the audience looks forward to the sight of Orlando wooing as a girl, a girl disguised as a boy – who in Shakespeare's day would actually have been a boy!

Act 4 Scene 1

Jaques wishes to be 'better acquainted' with Rosalind as the disguised Ganymede. In modern productions his request is sometimes played with homosexual undertones, hinting that Jaques has an erotic interest in this 'pretty youth'. But in this encounter between Jaques and Rosalind (the only time they talk together in the play) Shakespeare's interest is in melancholy. Jaques proudly agrees that he is 'a melancholy fellow', but Rosalind says that extremes of both melancholy or merriness are detestable.

You can find an account of what Elizabethans thought about melancholy on pages 72–4, 121. In a highly structured list, Jaques fashions his image by claiming his melancholy is more complex than anyone else's: the scholar's, musician's, courtier's, soldier's, lawyer's, lady's or lover's. He asserts his own melancholy is a special mixture, and is deepened by his thinking about his travels. Rosalind mocks his pretentiousness, and seems to ignore Orlando, whose greeting prompts Jaques to leave, complaining he cannot stand blank verse (see page 84).

Critics have detected in Rosalind's scorn Shakespeare's own mockery of the melancholy pose that many Elizabethan gentlemen affected as they spoke disdainfully and condescendingly of the foolishness they had seen everywhere on their travels. Rosalind's mocking farewell to Jaques reveals the affectations that these poseurs adopted: speaking in a foreign accent ('lisp'), wearing foreign clothes ('strange suits'), criticising England and seeming to hate their very birthplace or nationality ('nativity'), and blaming God for creating them melancholic:

> Farewell, Monsieur Traveller. Look you lisp and wear
> strange suits; disable all the benefits of your own country;
> be out of love with your nativity, and almost chide God for
> making you that countenance you are, or I will scarce
> think you have swam in a gondola.   *(lines 26–30)*

Rosalind then turns to Orlando and, fully in role as Ganymede playing Rosalind, berates him for his lateness. The episode that now follows (lines 31–176) is often called 'the wooing scene', in which Rosalind tricks Orlando into wooing her. He thinks he is talking to a young man, Ganymede, who has promised to act as Rosalind to cure him of his love. But Ganymede really is Rosalind, and she revels in the deception, teasing him and enjoying his love talk to her.

She doubts whether he is truly in love: any lover who is a fraction of a minute late is surely 'heart-whole' (not wounded by Cupid's arrow). She jokes about deceived husbands (her lines 48–50 about 'horns' were often cut in performance in the nineteenth century, being thought indecent), then joyously demands that Orlando woo her:

> Come, woo me, woo me; for now I am in a holiday
> humour and like enough to consent. What would you say
> to me now and I were your very, very Rosalind?
>
> *(lines 55–7)*

It is a daring performance, full of sexual ambivalence. Adding to Elizabethan audiences' ambiguous thrill of response to the episode was their knowledge that some of the words Rosalind uses as she teases Orlando possessed sexual meanings, as in two lines of Rosalind's that modern audiences find obscure:

> Marry, that should you if I were your mistress, or I
> should think my honesty ranker than my wit.   *(lines 66–7)*

The lines come after Rosalind says a lover should speak before he kisses, and Orlando asks who could be lost for words in front of his mistress. Rosalind's reply could mean that if she were his mistress, he would be tongue-tied, struck dumb by her purity ('honesty') rather than by her intelligence ('wit'). But a different meaning was possible for Elizabethans for whom 'honesty' could mean 'chastity', and 'wit' could mean 'sexual organ'. So Rosalind could be saying that Orlando would be soon out of his clothes ready for sexual intercourse, or she would think her chastity greater than her sex appeal. Today that possible meaning is lost, and an actress can only hint at it (if she wishes) by accompanying the words with some stage business.

Rosalind continues her teasing, declaring she will not have Orlando. Fully in the spirit of the love-pretending game, Orlando responds that he will therefore die for love. Onstage he often clutches his heart melodramatically as he speaks. But Rosalind lampoons his claim. She tells of famous mythological lovers: Troilus, the Trojan prince who loved the Greek Cressida, but 'had his brains dashed out' by Achilles; Leander, who loved Hero and swam the Hellespont each night to visit her, but was drowned in a storm:

> But these are all lies: men have died from time to time –
> and worms have eaten them – but not for love.   *(lines 84–5)*

It is a wonderfully deflating moment in which, through Rosalind's common sense, Shakespeare undercuts all the sentimentality of romantic love. Orlando struggles to continue the pretence of the love game, but Rosalind is always wittily in control. She steps up the intensity of the pretend wooing, ordering Celia (often, in performance, to Celia's evident discomfiture or annoyance) to step into role as priest to marry her to Orlando. For Elizabethans, the moment had added charge, because at that time, declaring an intent to marry in front of a witness created a binding contract. It is another breathtaking theatrical moment as, in spite of Celia's evident reluctance, the ceremony takes place:

CELIA   I cannot say the words.
ROSALIND   You must begin: 'Will you, Orlando –'
CELIA   Go to. – Will you, Orlando, have to wife this Rosalind?
ORLANDO   I will.
ROSALIND   Aye, but when?
ORLANDO   Why, now, as fast as she can marry us.
ROSALIND   Then you must say, 'I take thee, Rosalind, for wife.'
ORLANDO   I take thee, Rosalind, for wife.
ROSALIND   I might ask you for your commission, but I do take thee, Orlando, for my husband.

(lines 102–11)

Rosalind immediately jokes at her own forwardness ('There's a girl goes before the priest'), then responds to Orlando's claim he will love her 'For ever and a day.' Her images are a sardonic comment on how time sours marriages:

> Say a day without the 'ever'. No, no, Orlando: men are
> April when they woo, December when they wed; maids
> are May when they are maids, but the sky changes
> when they are wives.   *(lines 117–19)*

Rosalind now embarks on a dazzling display of wordplay. She warns of her future giddy behaviour, listing how capriciously she will behave when she is married, ranging from violent jealousy ('a Barbary cock-pigeon' was a fiercely protective male pigeon) to laughing like a hyena. In several speeches that were often cut in eighteenth- and nineteenth-century performances because they were thought indecent, she hints that wives and husbands are unfaithful (lines 129–41). Certainly, for Elizabethans there was a clear sexual joke running through the lines because she again plays upon 'wit', which, as noted above, carried sexual implications in Shakespeare's time.

Rosalind's exuberant flow of language leaves Orlando struggling. He tries to keep up, but can only make brief responses to her free-flowing imaginative teasing. It is a bravura performance, but its sheer overflow once provoked Peggy Ashcroft, a famous twentieth-century Rosalind, to comment 'Rosalind is a wonderful girl but I wish she didn't talk quite so much.' Whether Orlando finds it all too overwhelming is not certain, but he does suddenly find a reason to leave: to 'attend the duke at dinner'. Rosalind's response is another high-spirited display of friendly mockery as she extravagantly pretends to be a petulant, rejected woman:

> Aye, go your ways, go your ways. I knew what you would
> prove – my friends told me as much, and I thought no less.
> That flattering tongue of yours won me. 'Tis but one cast away,
> and so come, Death! Two o'clock is your hour?
>
> *(lines 146–9)*

In yet another outburst of verbal fireworks Rosalind warns Orlando not to be late. If he comes only a minute after the promised time she will think him 'the most pathetical break-promise, and the most hollow lover'. Orlando leaves, and Celia rebukes Rosalind, but Rosalind seems barely to listen. She can contain her passionate feelings no longer, and declares she is immeasurably deeply in love:

> O coz, coz, coz, my pretty little coz, that thou didst know how
> many fathom deep I am in love! But it cannot be sounded: my
> affection hath an unknown bottom, like the Bay of Portugal.
>
> *(lines 165–7)*

Celia expresses her scepticism, twisting Rosalind's image into one of fickleness: 'Or rather bottomless, that as fast as you pour affection in, it runs out.' At the scene's end Celia has only six lines to express her feelings. She criticises Rosalind for what she has said about women ('misused our sex'), and adapts the proverb 'It is the foul bird that defiles its own nest' (only bad women criticise other women).

Celia has a variety of possible ways to play this final episode. She has been presented as exasperated and disgruntled, as genuinely angry, as disconsolate and devastated at the thought that her former close relationship with Rosalind has ended, and as good-humoured, using a mocking style that conceals genuine affection. All these different interpretations have carried conviction in performance. Now, at the very end of the scene, Shakespeare gives her only three words to respond to yet another fervent declaration by Rosalind of her love for Orlando. How Celia delivers the words is a matter of how each actor playing the role sees the relationship between the two women at this moment in the play:

ROSALIND   I'll tell thee, Aliena, I cannot be out of the sight of
          Orlando. I'll go find a shadow and sigh till he come.
CELIA   And I'll sleep.   (lines 173–6)

Act 4 Scene 2

One function of this 'hunting scene' is to fill up the time before Orlando's promised return to Rosalind (between Scenes 1 and 3 two hours elapse in stage time). Another function is to add further reminders of the cuckoldry that was so much talked about in the previous scene: the Lords' song, with its 'The horn, the horn, the lusty horn', claims that it is man's destiny to be a cuckold. The scene also provides another insight into life in the forest as experienced by the exiled court. Previously they had talked of hunting. Now they are seen actually practising it. Another function is to reinforce the view of Jaques as a music-hating sceptic: ordering a song, he remarks, ''Tis no matter how it be in tune, so it make noise enough.'

On the page, the scene is very short: eight lines of dialogue and a ten-line song. Jaques proposes that the Lord who killed the deer be presented in triumph to Duke Senior, and the Lords sing about cuckoldry ('Take thou no scorn to wear the horn'). But in performance it often makes thrilling, impressive theatre as directors seize the opportunity offered. The scene has been played in all kinds of ways: as a celebration of hunting, as a very bloody pagan ritual, as a festival of forest life. In a production reported on page 104 Celia remained on stage from Scene 1. She slept, and the scene presented her nightmare of Rosalind being hunted, caught and raped.

Act 4 Scene 3

Two hours have passed from the end of Scene 1, but Orlando has not returned to Rosalind as he had promised. Celia suggests he has gone to hunt in the forest, and adds the mocking comment that he has fallen asleep. In some productions Celia's comment seems barbed, intended to further aggravate her friend's impatience. But the entrance of Silvius directs attention to another of the play's love relationships. Silvius tells that Phebe's letter contains an angry message, and his 'Pardon me, / I am but as a guiltless messenger', spoken with an air of wide-eyed innocence, often gets a big laugh in the theatre.

Rosalind reads the letter, and says that in it Phebe declares she could not love Ganymede even if he were the only man in the world ('as rare as phoenix'). The phoenix was a mythical bird. Only one was believed to be alive at any time. After 500 years it died, but was born again in fire. Its mention here is yet another way in which Shakespeare builds up the impression of the Forest of Arden as a mysterious place full of all kinds of wonders (see pages 123–4).

Rosalind seems annoyed at what she reads. She calls Silvius a fool, and launches an attack on Phebe ('she has a leathern hand'), claiming that her letter is full of insults. Rosalind's description of the contents of the letter, 'Ethiop words, blacker in their effect / Than in their countenance', is today regarded as offensive racist language. But in Elizabethan times such phrases expressed taken-for-granted beliefs: to Shakespeare's contemporaries, Ethiopians and black faces were the symbols of evil.

When Rosalind reads the letter aloud, it reveals that Phebe is passionately in love with Ganymede. She describes Ganymede as a god become man, who has conquered her heart. Phebe begs for a reply in a sealed letter from Ganymede, and Silvius is to deliver it. Silvius is understandably downcast at what he hears, and Celia pities him, but Rosalind expresses no such tender emotion and rebukes Silvius for being made so feeble by love. She dispatches him back to

Phebe with a stern message:

> Do you pity him? No, he deserves no pity. – Wilt thou love
> such a woman? What, to make thee an instrument and play
> false strains upon thee? Not to be endured! Well, go your way
> to her – for I see love hath made thee a tame snake – and say
> this to her: that if she love me, I charge her to love thee; if she
> will not, I will never have her, unless thou entreat for her.
>
> *(lines 63–8)*

Rosalind gives the 'tame snake' Silvius no opportunity to respond, ordering him away as Oliver enters.

Oliver, the brother who had treated Orlando so cruelly, was last seen in Act 3 Scene 1 being manhandled by Duke Frederick's officers. He was dispatched to capture Orlando, dead or alive. Now he seems a changed man, speaking courteously and recognising Rosalind and Celia as Ganymede and the shepherdess who had been described to him. He brings greetings from Orlando and presents Rosalind with a blood-stained handkerchief ('bloody napkin') sent by Orlando. Rosalind's reaction is a mixture of puzzlement, anticipation and fear: 'What must we understand by this?'

Oliver tells his story. Orlando, wandering through the forest, turning over pleasant and harsh memories in his mind ('Chewing the food of sweet and bitter fancy') saw an unkempt sleeping man threatened first by a snake, which then glided away, and then by a hungry lioness. Orlando recognised the man as his brother, who had treated him so vilely. Twice he turned away, thinking to leave his wicked brother to be eaten by the beast, but brotherly love prevailed and he fought and killed the lion.

The story Oliver tells is improbably melodramatic, but it is a typical example of the genre of pastoral romance in which all kinds of improbabilities can occur (see page 62). Forests can contain snakes and lions as well as deer and sheep, and heroes can conquer the wildest of beasts with their bare hands. In this world of pastoral romance the snake and the lion have symbolic significance as images of the deceit and brutality which Oliver once practised, but which now will be rejected and conquered.

Oliver's story is a tale of forgiveness and reconciliation, telling how brotherly love triumphed over the unnaturalness of brotherly hate.

Some critics have seen the episode as expressing the heart of the moral dimension of the play: Orlando twice was about to abandon his cruel brother to a savage death, but 'kindness' and 'nature' overcame any feeling of resentment and revenge, and Orlando risked his own life to save his brother. That action brings about Oliver's 'conversion' (change to goodness). He reveals he was the sleeping man, and, to the amazed Celia and Rosalind, tells of his moral transformation:

CELIA   Are you his brother?
ROSALIND   Was't you he rescued?
CELIA   Was't you that did so oft contrive to kill him?
OLIVER   'Twas I, but 'tis not I. I do not shame
     To tell you what I was, since my conversion
     So sweetly tastes, being the thing I am.   *(lines 128–32)*

Oliver's "Twas I, but 'tis not I' and 'being the thing I am' show how Shakespeare often expresses fundamental truths in the simplest of language. In *Twelfth Night* and *Othello* both Viola and Iago say 'I am not what I am' to make a statement quite opposite to Oliver's. They are practising deception; their outward appearance does not match their inner nature. But Oliver, in the tradition of the changed villain of pastoral romance, declares he is now without guile, he truly is good.

Rosalind is desperate to learn the meaning of the blood-stained handkerchief, and for news of Orlando. But Oliver makes her wait ('By and by'). Some critics think that Oliver is totally caught up with Celia, with whom he has fallen in love. Others are confident that Oliver sees through Rosalind's disguise as Ganymede. But those are interpretations that every production decides whether or not to show onstage; Shakespeare leaves the possibilities open to performance and has Oliver continue his story.

Oliver relates how each brother tearfully told the other his story, then were given hospitality by Duke Senior. Orlando showed that the lion had wounded his arm, he had fainted, then recovered and sent Oliver with the blood-stained handkerchief to Ganymede. Looking again at the bloody napkin, Rosalind faints, recovers, and pretends her swooning is a pretence. The episode gives actors rich opportunity for comedy as Rosalind's disguise comes close to discovery:

- Celia's 'There is more in it' often provokes audience laughter, because the audience knows what that 'more' is.
- Oliver sometimes begins to unbutton Ganymede's doublet to give 'him' air. Rosalind's startled response provokes Oliver's 'Look, he recovers', again causing audience laughter.
- Rosalind sometimes gets close to giving her disguise away, for example when she hears that Orlando, fainting, called out her name (line 144), and when she exclaims plaintively 'I would I were at home.'
- Celia also comes close to giving the game away. Trying to revive Rosalind, she calls her 'Cousin'.

Rosalind's repeated insistence that her fainting was a 'counterfeit' is often regarded very suspiciously by Oliver, and Rosalind goes to greater and greater lengths to persuade him she ('he') was only faking the faint. Each one of her seemingly casual protests, full of assumed masculine bravado, amuses the audience, who are fully in on the secret: 'I pray you tell your brother how well I counterfeited. Heigh-ho!' (lines 160–1); 'Counterfeit, I assure you' (line 164); 'I should have been a woman by right' (line 166). She leaves promising to make up a message for Orlando, but still desperate to create the impression that she simply imitated swooning at the sight of blood:

> I shall devise something. But I pray you commend
> my counterfeiting to him. Will you go?   *(lines 171–2)*

Act 4: Critical review

Scene 1, the 'wooing scene', is full of highly charged erotic ambiguity. The disguised Rosalind is eagerly demanding love; Orlando must pretend to declare his love to another 'male' – who actually is the female he loves. In Shakespeare's time the audience would see onstage one man protesting his love to another – a relationship strictly forbidden and severely punished in real life. But in the world of the play Rosalind gets what she wants: the man she loves declares his love and marries her.

Many critics claim that the effect of the wooing scene is to weaken the bond between the two women. In the early scenes of the play, Celia had quite a large speaking role. Now, as Rosalind plays her love scenes with Orlando, Celia has less and less to say. Here she only gets the chance, probably reluctantly, to act as 'priest' to 'marry' the lovers. In performance she often shows her displeasure at what is going on. One feminist interpretation is that Celia feels that Arden, like the court, is a man's world, in which her best friend has only to dress as a man to lord it over others.

Scene 2, the 'hunting scene', returns to an all-male world where horns and cuckoldry were standing jokes. Shakespeare may have written the scene because he knew that hunting scenes held great appeal for his audiences (he had already used them in *Titus Andronicus*, *The Taming of the Shrew*, *Love's Labour's Lost*, *A Midsummer Night's Dream* and *The Merry Wives of Windsor*). Such scenes had also become an accepted element of the pastoral tradition that so influences the play. In this genre it was an expectation that plays and stories should include a hunt, music and singing, and a ritual presentation of a trophy (such as the antlers of a deer) to the huntsman who had made the kill.

Scene 3, with Oliver's improbable tale of his conversion to goodness through Orlando's rescue of him from the exotic dangers of the forest, is typical of the pastoral romance tradition. Rosalind's fainting at the sight of blood, and her insistence that she was only 'feigning', is yet another example of the play's concern with the difference between reality and appearance.

Act 5 Scene 1

The scene begins in the middle of a conversation. Audrey regrets that Sir Oliver Martext did not marry her to Touchstone. It seems that the two have only just come from their meeting with Sir Oliver (Act 3 Scene 4), but there has been a great deal of stage action since then. Perhaps this is another example of Shakespeare suggesting that, in the Forest of Arden, time is of little significance.

What seems more certain, however, is that in this short scene Shakespeare is concerned to show yet another aspect of love in the shape of the rustic William. He proves no real opponent for Touchstone, who mocks him unmercifully throughout the scene, moving from false courtesy to threat of violence.

The sophisticated Touchstone increasingly bamboozles the ignorant William with impressive-sounding but empty language. William does little more than respond briefly to Touchstone's questions. Even his replies expose him to ridicule, especially his incongruous claim 'Aye, sir, I have a pretty wit.' It simply prompts Touchstone to a display of pretentious logic which onstage is also usually seen as a response to William standing open-mouthed and wide-eyed:

> The heathen philosopher, when he had a desire to eat a grape, would open his lips when he put it into his mouth, meaning thereby that grapes were made to eat and lips to open.
>
> *(lines 29–31)*

Even though some critics have attempted to identify Touchstone's 'heathen philosopher', it seems a fairly pointless exercise, as Touchstone (or rather, Shakespeare) is probably just letting his imagination run, and this is, after all, Arden, a place that licenses fancy. Touchstone is concerned to prove both his intellectual superiority over William and that he has a better claim to Audrey. So, in a mixture of logic and elaborate wordplay, he first proves that he is *ipse* ('he himself' in Latin: the man who must marry Audrey), then orders William to give up his wooing, and then threatens him with all kinds of punishments. Touchstone's translation of words and phrases into ordinary language ('vulgar', 'boorish', 'common') can be seen as a further way in which Shakespeare parodies the debate between court and country:

Therefore, you clown, abandon, which is in the vulgar,
'leave the society', which in the boorish is 'company', of this
female, which in the common is 'woman': which together
is 'abandon the society of this female'

(lines 41–4)

Touchstone is determined to show the supremacy of the court, and he
elaborately lists ways in which he will dispose of William. But in one
production, as Touchstone finished his threats, William seized him
and almost strangled him until Audrey pleaded, 'Do, good William.'
However, most productions show Touchstone winning a very easy
victory over a dull but benign opponent, who gains a good deal of
audience sympathy in performance, as he leaves bewildered but
peacefully. As a new character, appearing only once at this late stage
of the play, William's dramatic function seems to be to further
illustrate the 'court versus country' theme, but other suggestions have
been made:

- to provide yet another view of love;
- to provide a contrast with the previous scene;
- a private joke on Shakespeare's own name (did he enjoy portraying
  himself as an ignorant rustic?);
- because the original actor playing William was loved by
  Elizabethan audiences.

Act 5 Scene 2

The previous scene ends with Touchstone urging, 'Trip, Audrey, trip,
Audrey.' After the sight of these two strangely matched lovers,
Shakespeare now provides news of yet another pair of lovers in the
forest. Orlando seems amazed to learn that Oliver fell instantly in love
with Celia, and she has consented to marry him. Oliver's conversion
to goodness and humility now seems complete. He promises to give
Orlando all his inheritance (forgetting that Duke Frederick had seized
all his lands in Act 3 Scene 1), and declares that, married to Celia,
whom he thinks of as Aliena, a poor shepherdess, he desires only to
spend the rest of his life with her, and be a shepherd in the forest.

Orlando agrees to all of Oliver's wishes, and proposes the wedding
takes place tomorrow. Shakespeare now provides an ambiguous
moment as Oliver, departing, calls Rosalind 'fair sister'. In some

productions Oliver's delivery of the line suggests that he knows that Ganymede is Rosalind in disguise.

Rosalind's confirmation that Oliver and Celia instantly fell in love uses a language style that matches the rapidity of falling in love at first sight. Just as Orlando and Oliver had done in their first speeches in the scene, she piles item on item, event on event, in rapid succession.

Educated Elizabethans would recognise her speech as an example of *gradatio*, a rhetorical device that students learned at school. Today, it is usually sufficient to identify the technique as a 'list' (see page 81). Rosalind begins with two examples of speed: how two rams rush at each other in a fight, and how Julius Caesar boasted of a rapid victory, saying '"I came, saw, and overcame"' (I came, I saw, I conquered). She then describes the development of Oliver and Celia's love as a rapid procession of steps:

> For your brother and my sister no sooner met but they looked;
> no sooner looked, but they loved; no sooner loved, but they
> sighed; no sooner sighed, but they asked one another the
> reason; no sooner knew the reason, but they sought the
> remedy; and in these degrees have they made a pair of stairs
> to marriage
>
> *(lines 25–30)*

Orlando's reflection that Oliver's joy at marriage will match his own sadness in not having Rosalind has become a well-known saying: 'how bitter a thing it is to look into happiness through another man's eyes'. He feels he can no longer continue the playful love game with Ganymede, pretending she is Rosalind: 'I can live no longer by thinking.' His words are the cue for Rosalind to propose her plan to bring about a happy ending.

Some critics have argued that Rosalind's manner and language change as she claims special powers and promises Orlando that he will marry his Rosalind tomorrow. Such critics see her speaking first in a formal, businesslike tone as she tells Orlando she wishes to help him. Lines 42–6 have, in fact, proved notoriously difficult to understand. They mean something like: 'I say that you are intelligent, not to get you to think well of me; the only esteem I want is from helping you, not to improve my own reputation.' But what she then goes on to say offers rich opportunities for Rosalind to speak in a ritualistic manner to bring out the uncanny, magical nature of her words:

> Believe then, if you please, that I can do strange things. I have, since I was three year old, conversed with a magician, most profound in his art, and yet not damnable. If you do love Rosalind so near the heart as your gesture cries it out, when your brother marries Aliena shall you marry her. I know into what straits of fortune she is driven, and it is not impossible to me, if it appear not inconvenient to you, to set her before your eyes tomorrow, human as she is, and without any danger.
>
> *(lines 46–53)*

In performance, Orlando usually reacts with wonder to Rosalind's words, as she once more claims to be a magician who does not practise the black magic which would imperil her life. That mood of mystery and ritual deepens with the entry of Silvius and Phebe and the switch to highly patterned and rhythmic verse. The responses of each character resemble a church litany as, in a thrice-repeated chorus, each one echoes Silvius' declaration of love:

SILVIUS   And so am I for Phebe.
PHEBE   And I for Ganymede.
ORLANDO   And I for Rosalind.
ROSALIND   And I for no woman   *(lines 68–71, 73–6, 82–5)*

After yet another echoing refrain as each lover complains 'If this be so, why blame you me to love you?', Rosalind breaks the ritualistic spell. Her tart image of the monotony of the repetitions usually evokes audience laughter:

> Pray you no more of this, 'tis like the howling of Irish
> wolves against the moon.   *(lines 91–2)*

The mood of wonder and the incantatory style of speaking is modified, but is still maintained as Rosalind briskly gives orders for them all to meet tomorrow, when their desires will be fulfilled. Her highly patterned speech promises that each will be satisfied, and she too will be married, but to no woman (she is of course speaking as

Ganymede). The final four lines of the scene once again have lovers responding like church members to a priest's command:

ROSALIND   So, fare you well: I have left you commands.
SILVIUS   I'll not fail, if I live.
PHEBE   Nor I.
ORLANDO   Nor I.   *(lines 100–3)*

Act 5 Scene 3

After the previous scene's preparations for three imminent weddings, the audience now see a fourth pair of lovers, Touchstone and Audrey, also looking forward to marriage tomorrow. Scene 3 seems to have two dramatic purposes: first to mark the passage of time between Scenes 2 and 4 (between Rosalind's instructions to prepare for marriage, and the ceremony in the final scene); second, in the Pages' song, to echo the play's theme of love, now that all four lovers are preparing for marriage:

> It was a lover and his lass,
> With a hey, and a ho, and a hey nonny-no   *(lines 13–14)*

The music composed in 1600 by Thomas Morley is still often used in stage productions. The song tells of springtime as the time for young lovers, and of the brevity of human life ('life was but a flower'). It urges that present happiness should be seized and enjoyed ('take the present time') when the season of springtime is perfect for lovers ('the prime').

The theme of the song is *carpe diem*, a Latin phrase meaning 'seize the day', taken from the Roman poet Horace (68–5 BC). *Carpe diem* has been a topic of literature and drama for over 2,000 years. It is still much used today in all forms of culture. For example, it is the theme of the film *Dead Poets' Society*; and much popular music in effect urges listeners to 'gather ye rosebuds while ye may'.

Onstage, the Pages' singing usually creates a delightful interlude, but Touchstone is unimpressed. He thinks it a waste of time to listen to 'such a foolish song', a reaction that resembles that of Jaques when he listened to the songs in Act 2 Scene 5. Touchstone leaves, dismissing the Pages' efforts with 'God mend your voices.' Perhaps Shakespeare was excusing the breaking voices of his actors, or perhaps he was, through Touchstone, ridiculing the sentiment of the song ('there was no great matter in the ditty'). No one knows, and today the song is judged as dramatically apt in how well it expresses happiness through love.

Act 5 Scene 4

The final scene of the play begins in doubt, with Orlando uncertain whether Ganymede (Rosalind) can fulfil the promises he made. Rosalind enters and asks for patience whilst she gets each character to confirm their own promise:

- that Duke Senior will give his daughter in marriage to Orlando;
- that Orlando will marry Rosalind;
- that if Phebe refuses to marry Ganymede, she will marry Silvius;
- that Silvius will marry Phebe.

Onstage, Rosalind then often delivers her orders as a kind of magical spell or incantation, commanding that each character keep his or her word. She leaves, and the exchange between Orlando and Duke Senior seems to confirm that Rosalind's disguise as Ganymede is still intact, even though both men say that 'this shepherd boy' reminded them of Rosalind. Up to this moment the dialogue has been in verse, a form that suits the somewhat formal, ritualistic tone of the exchanges. But with the entry of Touchstone and Audrey Shakespeare switches to prose, perhaps to signify the return to comedy (but see page 82).

Touchstone boasts of his skills as a courtier, claiming he is practised in dancing (a 'measure' is a stately dance), flattery, diplomacy and deceit ('politic'), false friendship ('smooth'), and non-payment of bills (he has ruined – 'undone' – three tailors). His claim that he has had four quarrels and almost fought a duel over one fascinates Jaques, who demands to know more. But Touchstone does not immediately explain. Rather, he declares he too wishes to be married, because Audrey's ugliness conceals inner virtues. Touchstone's comparisons of Audrey ('an ill-favoured thing, sir, but mine own') with the wealthy miser in a poor house and the pearl in an oyster echoes the theme of appearance and reality. Audrey may not be outwardly attractive, but she has inner qualities.

Jaques persists in his demand to know how Touchstone avoided a quarrel by use of 'the seventh cause'. At last Touchstone explains, pausing only to order Audrey 'Bear your body more seeming, Audrey', a remark which often causes an explosion of audience laughter – just how might she have been behaving? Touchstone lists the sequence of insults that lead up to a duel, and explains how to avoid the duel with an 'if'. Shakespeare is satirising the manuals on duelling and the handbooks on correct behaviour for courtiers which were written during the Elizabethan age (most notably Castiglione's *The Courtier*, 1561). Such etiquette books were about how to behave in a duel when one's honour had been insulted. A 1594 handbook for duellists actually included a section titled 'the giving and receiving of the lie'.

Jaques is delighted and asks for a recapitulation that names each stage of the quarrel. Touchstone obliges, and his introduction specifically refers to the etiquette manuals of the times: 'we quarrel in print, by the book – as you have books for good manners.' He tells how cowardly courtiers use language to avoid having to fight, listing the seven stages of a quarrel, and showing that after all the formal exchanges of insults, actual violence can be avoided with an 'if'.

Touchstone's two lengthy explanations not only satirise contemporary handbooks on etiquette. They give the actor the opportunity for a bravura performance, and some Touchstones name the degrees of the quarrel without pausing for breath – a feat that often evokes applause from both the onstage and auditorium audience. But the interlude also has a very practical dramatic function. It gives Rosalind and Celia time to change out of their disguises as Ganymede and Aliena. They now appear as themselves, accompanied by Hymen, the Greek and Roman god of marriage.

The entry of Hymen, god of marriage, is a great moment of theatre. In Elizabethan times the episode may have been staged as a masque. Masques became increasingly popular in Shakespeare's lifetime. They were spectacular court entertainments which drew imaginatively on classical mythology to present gods and goddesses. They used elaborate scenery and costumes, and were filled with music, poetry and dance. Masques revelled in visual effects, often using complex stage machinery and lighting to create striking illusions. In one Jacobean masque, Hymen was dressed in a yellow robe, with a wreath of roses on his head, carrying a flaming torch.

In the nineteenth century, productions similarly seized the opportunity for theatrical display, sometimes having Hymen accompanied by a host of shepherds and shepherdesses and attendants strewing flowers. Modern productions occasionally also stage a spectacular, 'magical' entry for Hymen, emphasising his unearthly, mysterious nature. But often he is recognisable as a character in the play (for example Corin, Adam or Amiens), obviously in disguise, and obviously not intended as a god with mystical powers. But however Hymen is presented, as he asks the Duke to receive Rosalind and join her in marriage to Orlando, the rhyming verse of his language together with its religious vocabulary create a formal, ritualistic effect:

> Then is there mirth in heaven,
> When earthly things made even
> Atone together.
> Good duke, receive thy daughter;
> Hymen from heaven brought her,
> Yea, brought her hither
> That thou mightst join her hand with his,
> Whose heart within his bosom is. *(lines 93–100)*

In an equally formal style Rosalind gives herself to her father and to Orlando. They respond in similar style, echoing each other's words as they acknowledge her as truly Rosalind. So too does Phebe as she bids farewell to her love for Ganymede, recognising she has mistaken 'him' for a man. Onstage, the reaction of Silvius shows that he suddenly realises that Phebe may marry him after all – as does she. In performance the entire stage action often 'freezes' momentarily at this point to highlight the sense of wonder felt by everyone as they sense the happiness the reunitings will bring. Hymen interrupts:

> Peace, ho: I bar confusion,
> 'Tis I must make conclusion
> Of these most strange events. *(lines 109–11)*

And he proceeds to do just that, ordaining the four marriages and addressing each couple in turn.

His line 'If truth holds true contents' (114) has puzzled generations of critics and scholars. Malcolm Evans has suggested it has at least 168 possible interpretations (see page 106). Two possibilities are 'if revealing who Ganymede and Aliena really are brings genuine happiness', or 'if the couples remain true to their vows'. The Hymen episode ends with a song celebrating marriage and fertility. It is sometimes sung by Amiens, sometimes by everyone onstage. At its conclusion Duke Senior welcomes Celia as his 'Even daughter' (probably meaning 'even as my own daughter'), and Phebe accepts Silvius. All seems complete, the play is very close to its end, but Shakespeare has more wonders to unfold that both celebrate and satirise the tradition of pastoral romance.

Jaques de Boys, brother of Orlando and Oliver, enters. He has not been heard of since the very beginning of the play when Orlando spoke of him succeeding brilliantly in his studies. Now he brings news. The tyrant Duke Frederick had mustered an army to march on Arden to kill Duke Senior. But meeting 'an old religious man' Frederick converted to goodness and penitence. He now gives back the crown to Duke Senior and restores all the lands he had stolen to their rightful owners.

The news of Duke Frederick's sudden and improbable conversion is yet another example of the unlikely surprises that the literary pastoral romance tradition legitimises. As page 64 shows, the stories in that tradition delighted in happy endings in which order was restored with reconciliations, conversions to goodness and other improbabilities, forgiveness, marriages, and the prospect of harmony for individuals and society.

Duke Senior, restored to his title and possessions, welcomes Jaques de Boys, and acknowledges Orlando, through his marriage to Rosalind, as the heir to the dukedom. He proposes his exiled companions leave Arden for the court, where everyone will be restored to the status and wealth they enjoyed before they came to the forest. He orders revelry:

> Play, music – and you, brides and bridegrooms all,
> With measure heaped in joy to th'measures fall.

(lines 162–3)

But before the music and dancing can begin, Jaques declines to participate in the merry-making. He resolves to join Duke Frederick in abandoning court life, and to learn from the secluded life of a 'convertite' (religious convert). He predicts honour and success to all except Touchstone, whose marriage will, he claims, last only for two months. Jaques' dissent injects a serious note into the closing festivities, but his action is typical of the melancholy man of Elizabethan England that he represents: he must reject both dancing and 'pastime'. He leaves, the awkward moment passes, and Duke Senior is determined on celebration:

> Proceed, proceed. – We will begin these rites
> As we do trust they'll end, in true delights.　　*(lines 181–2)*

In most productions the dancing is unequivocally joyful, a blithe celebration that really does express the hoped-for 'true delights' that will follow the weddings. Usually the lovers pair up as they dance, and as the stage empties, each couple also leaves hand-in-hand or in some way that the director feels symbolises their future relationship (Touchstone and Audrey sometimes begin quarrelling). Rosalind and Orlando are last to leave, and it seems that the performance has ended. But Shakespeare has something more in mind. Rosalind turns back, and, alone onstage, addresses the audience directly in the Epilogue, asking them to approve the play with their applause.

This is one of the very few times that a female character spoke an epilogue (as Rosalind acknowledges in 'It is not the fashion to see the lady the Epilogue'). More significantly, it is the only time that an actor in a Shakespeare play directly acknowledges that he is a man playing a woman's part. Line 13, 'If I were a woman,' is a reminder that in Shakespeare's time all actors were male, and Rosalind was probably played by a boy or very young man.

As You Like It is a comedy that celebrates sexual ambiguity through Rosalind's cross-dressing. The ambiguity is heightened when it is revealed that the girl playing a boy is indeed a male. Some critics claim that the onstage admission of being a male enhanced the erotic effect of the moment on some male members of Elizabethan and Jacobean audiences as they were told that the actor playing Rosalind would kiss them if he really were a woman. Today nearly all Rosalinds are female, and line 13 is often changed (for example to 'If I were among you'). But female Rosalinds sometimes use stage business to break the illusion of the play, and to return the audience to the everyday world. For example in one production, as Rosalind spoke, she removed her wedding dress to reveal she was wearing a modern sweater, trainers and jeans. The time for illusion was over.

Act 5: Critical review

Act 5 is traditionally seen as drawing together major themes of the play: love, court versus country, and appearance and reality. William's brief appearance in Scene 1 is a tongue-tied addition to Shakespeare's catalogue of lovers. Oliver's declaration that he and Celia fell instantly in love provides the play with a fourth pair of contrasting lovers. The final scene seems the very model of how a comedy should end: in reconciliation, merriment and marriage.

The play's preoccupation with the contrast between court and country is evident in Scene 1 as the sophisticated Touchstone runs verbal rings around the hapless William. But if the court wins there, Touchstone's bravura performance in the final scene, as he lists the seven stages of a quarrel, can be interpreted as satirising the over-sophistication of courtiers.

Perhaps the most telling feature in Shakespeare's ironic scrutiny of the court versus country debate is the decision of Duke Senior that he, the lovers and his exiled companions will return to court. The time for playing at foresters or shepherds is over and a more attractive and comfortable world beckons. Only the melancholy Jaques refuses to return, but even his wish to learn from the reformed Duke Frederick represents a fashionable attitude of the times: that of the sardonic malcontent.

The theme of appearance and reality takes on a mysterious, ritual dimension in Act 5 as Rosalind practises the magician's art. For modern audiences the entry of Hymen might seem entirely unexpected: the intrusion of the supernatural into the human world. But the genre of the play, pastoral romance, justifies such marvels. The fictional world of Arden is a place where anything can happen, however improbable.

As Rosalind drops her disguise, the reality behind Ganymede's appearance seems to resolve all confusions. Phebe's affections switch to Silvius, and Orlando gains his Rosalind. But Shakespeare has a final surprise in store as Rosalind reveals 'her' gender in the Epilogue: it is a male player who invites the audience to bid him farewell. Gender, like Arden itself, exists in the imagination and desires of men and women.

Contexts

The hugely enjoyable film *Shakespeare in Love* portrays a popular belief about the source of Shakespeare's creativity. It shows him suffering from 'writer's block', unable to put pen to paper, with no idea of how to write his next play. But all is resolved when he meets a beautiful young girl. His love for her sparks an overwhelming flow of creative energy – and he writes *Romeo and Juliet*!

It is an attractive idea, and the film presents it delightfully, but the truth of the matter is far more complex. Like every other writer, Shakespeare was influenced by many factors other than his own personal experience. The society of his time, its practices, beliefs and language in political and economic affairs, culture and religion, were the raw materials on which his imagination worked.

This section identifies the contexts from which *As You Like It* emerged: the wide range of different influences which fostered the creativity of Shakespeare as he wrote the play. These contexts ensured that *As You Like It* is full of all kinds of reminders of everyday life, and the familiar knowledge, assumptions, beliefs and values of Shakespeare's England.

What did Shakespeare write?

Scholars generally agree that Shakespeare wrote *As You Like It* sometime around 1599–1600. What was the play that Shakespeare wrote and his audiences heard? No one knows for certain because his original script has not survived, nor have any handwritten amendments he might subsequently have made. So what is the origin of the text of the play you are studying? *As You Like It* was first published in 1623 (seven years after Shakespeare's death) in the volume known as the First Folio, which contains 36 of his plays.

Today, all editions of *As You Like It* are based on the First Folio version. But the edition of the play you are using will vary in many minor respects from other editions. That is because although every editor of the play uses the Folio version, each one makes a multitude of different judgements about such matters as spelling, punctuation, stage directions (entrances and exits, asides, etc.), scene locations and other features.

So the text of *As You Like It* is not as stable as you might think. This is no reason for dismay, but rather an opportunity to think about how the differences reflect what actually happens in performance. Every production, on stage or film, cuts, adapts and amends the text to present its own unique version of *As You Like It*. This Guide follows the New Cambridge edition of the play (also used in Cambridge School Shakespeare).

What did Shakespeare read?

Shakespeare's genius lay in his ability to transform what he read into gripping drama. This section is therefore about the influence of genre: the literary contexts of *As You Like It* (you might think of it as about what critics today call 'intertextuality': the way texts influence each other). It identifies the stories and dramatic conventions that fired Shakespeare's imagination as he wrote *As You Like It*.

Shakespeare's major inspiration for *As You Like It* was a story by Thomas Lodge: 'Rosalynde, Euphues Golden Legacy'. Lodge had written his tale on a sea voyage to the Canary Islands, and published it in 1590. He based it on a fourteenth-century narrative poem, *Tale of Gamelyn*, and it was one of many stories and plays of the pastoral romance tradition (see page 62) very popular in Shakespeare's time. Lodge's book enjoyed wide readership: ten editions were published over 50 years. Just as he had done with *Romeo and Juliet*, Shakespeare turned a widely known and much-liked fictional romantic tale into successful drama. The following summary of 'Rosalynde' (with the names of Shakespeare's characters added in brackets) shows how closely Shakespeare followed Lodge's plot:

> Sir John of Bordeaux dies, leaving three sons. The youngest son, Rosader (Orlando) is kept in poverty by the oldest son, Saladyne (Oliver). Rosader rebels, and Saladyne plots that a wrestler kill Rosader. But Rosader kills the wrestler. Rosalynde (Rosalind) watches the fight and falls in love with Rosader. She is the daughter of the rightful king, Gerismond (Duke Senior), who has been overthrown by Torismond (Duke Frederick) and now lives in exile. She sends Rosader a jewel and he sends a poem in return.

> Saladyne again plots to kill Rosader, who flees to the Forest of Arden together with his loyal servant Adam Spencer (Adam).

He and Adam, nearly dead from hunger, receive hospitality from the exiled king Gerismond.

Rosalynde is banished from court by Torismond, who fears she may threaten his possession of the crown. Alinda (Celia), daughter of the wrongful king, protests, and she too is banished. The two women flee to the Forest of Arden. They disguise themselves as Ganymede and Aliena. In the forest they overhear a young shepherd (Silvius) telling an old shepherd (Corin) of his unrequited love for Phoebe (Phebe), a shepherdess. Aliena buys the cottage and sheep of Corin's master, and she and Ganymede set up as shepherds.

Rosader writes love poems to Rosalynde, carving them on trees. Rosalynde, teased by Aliena, realises she loves Rosader, and, as Ganymede, encourages him to woo her as if she were Rosalynde. Aliena conducts a mock wedding of Rosalynde and Rosader.

Rosalynde criticises Phoebe for failing to love Silvius, but Phoebe falls in love with her, believing she is the male Ganymede. Phoebe sends a love letter to Ganymede, but eventually agrees to end her love if reason can persuade her.

Meanwhile Saladyne, who has been punished and banished by Torismond, has repented of his evil deeds against Rosader, and now seeks him in Arden. He sleeps, and just as he is about to be attacked by a lion, Rosader rescues him. The two brothers are reconciled, and together they defeat an attack on Aliena by a band of outlaws. Saladyne and Aliena gradually fall in love.

Rosalynde organises three weddings through a promise of 'magic'. She drops her disguise as Ganymede and is reunited with her father, the exiled king. The three marriages take place in church, and amid the celebrations the brother of Rosander and Saladyne appears with news of support for Gerismond against the usurper. Torismond is slain, and Gerismond regains his throne. All ends happily.

The alterations and additions that Shakespeare made in dramatising Lodge's fictional romance are evident:

- He added extra characters: a cynical and a comic commentator (Jaques and Touchstone), another pair of lovers (Touchstone and Audrey) and a simple rustic (William).
- He greatly reduces the violence of the story. Nobody gets killed in *As You Like It*.
- He increases the emphasis on family relationships by turning the unrelated Torismond and Gerismond into the brothers Duke Frederick and Duke Senior (and so making Celia and Rosalind cousins).
- He has the usurping brother repent at the end, as Frederick, converted by 'an old religious man', undergoes a spiritual transformation and abandons his armed expedition to kill his brother.
- He makes the women's roles more complex: for example, Celia chooses exile, falls instantly in love, and seems to become exasperated with Rosalind's 'wooing' as Ganymede: 'You have simply misused our sex'. Rosalind becomes far wittier and more appealing than in Lodge.
- He changes the tone and style from conventional moralising to high comedy that is multilayered and often ironic.
- He intensifies the anatomising of love. By having each pair of lovers speaking in different styles, he shows the wide variety of love's expression, sincerities and absurdities.
- He rearranges and concentrates the action, most notably in bringing together a variety of love scenes in the centre of the play.

As You Like It can also be considered in the context of Shakespeare's writing career. He had already explored a number of its elements in earlier plays. For example, *As You Like It* opens like the beginning of a tragedy, and he had begun other comedies in the same way: *The Comedy of Errors* begins with a man condemned to death; in the first scene of *A Midsummer Night's Dream* a daughter is threatened with death for defying her father; and *The Merchant of Venice* starts with the melancholy of Antonio, who later puts his life at risk for his friend. A sombre and menacing strain seems a characteristic of Shakespeare's comedies before *As You Like It*, and would appear also in *Twelfth Night*, which was shortly to follow around 1601.

Similarly, Shakespeare had already dramatised the character of a feisty and intelligent woman who drives much of the action of the play, and who is clearly the equal of any man: Julia in *The Two Gentlemen of Verona*, Katherine in *The Taming of the Shrew*, Rosaline in *Love's Labour's Lost*, Portia in *The Merchant of Venice*, Beatrice in *Much Ado About Nothing*, and Mistress Ford and Mistress Page in *The Merry Wives of Windsor*. Two of those resourceful women (Julia and Portia) had disguised themselves as a male, and Viola in *Twelfth Night* was shortly to do the same. All can be seen as part of Shakespeare's dramatic imagination as he created Rosalind.

As You Like It can also be seen as part of the development of Shakespeare's use of 'festivity'. In his festive comedies, understanding is gained, love triumphs and reconciliations are achieved through 'holiday': a time, place or atmosphere in which conventional values and behaviour are turned upside down (see page 91). The Forest of Arden is just such a place, and something of its origin can be seen in the literary tradition of pastoral romance.

The pastoral romance tradition

As Shakespeare wrote *As You Like It*, he was much influenced by what is now called the pastoral romance tradition. It portrayed rural life as an ideal world of innocence and freedom. It was a world into which kings and queens and courtiers could escape. Disguised as shepherds and shepherdesses, they could enjoy the tranquillity and harmony of country life.

The tradition was (and still is) made up of two major strands: 'Pastoral' and 'Romance'.

Pastoral. Pastoral was a literature and drama that idealised nature and rural life. It presented the country as far superior to the city, a place of escape. The country taught moral lessons (expressed by Duke Senior as 'books in the running brooks, / Sermons in stones, and good in everything.'). In the country, remote from the town, human nature could be changed for good. Some modern critics express pastoral as a binary opposition between civilisation and rudeness, between urban sophistication and uneducated rustic simplicity. It has also been called 'the dispute between Velvet Breeches and Cloth Breeches'.

The pastoral tradition has a history that stretches back over 2,000 years to the Greek poet Theocritus (316–260 BC). He and other writers of classical antiquity created a 'golden world' of peaceful and harmonious country life. This rural idyll was peopled by beautiful shepherdesses and shepherds (*pastor* in Latin means shepherd). They were poets, philosophers and lovers – and were often aristocrats in disguise as humble country folk.

The pastoral tradition took many forms. Shakespeare would certainly have heard it in folk tales such as that of Robin Hood and his Merry Men in Sherwood Forest. He would also have read some of its most famous literary expressions, written in his own lifetime. These included Sir Philip Sidney's *Arcadia* (1590), and Edmund Spenser's *The Shepherd's Calendar* (1579) and *The Faerie Queene* (1590–6). He would also have seen some of the many popular dramatisations of the genre in the theatre.

Romance. The romance tradition largely derives from stories of love and chivalry, which were very popular in the Middle Ages, for example, tales of King Arthur, the *Song of Rolande*, *Roman de la Rose* and Chaucer's *Knight's Tale*. It dealt with the trials of young knights, and presented two views of love: courtly and romantic. Courtly love was sexless and idealised. It put women 'on a pedestal' and worshipped them as unattainable goddesses. Only by long devotion, many trials and much suffering could a man win his ideal woman, the 'fair, cruel maid' of literature. Romantic love was also idealised and non-sexual, but it included 'love at first sight'. Marriage was seen as its natural result.

These two traditions, 'pastoral' and 'romance', increasingly merged into pastoral romance. Indeed, Sidney's and Spenser's work, described above as 'pastoral', can equally be thought of as 'romance'. Pastoral romance literature thus typically included the following features (with a brief indication in brackets of how they appear in *As You Like It*):

- Shepherds: lovesick shepherds, scornful shepherdesses (Silvius and Phebe).
- Forests: where magical transformations occur, and true love flourishes after rigorous testing; a place of deposed rulers, merry men, kindly outlaws and magicians (the Forest of Arden, Duke Senior's exiled court).
- Journeys, adventures and learning: a young knight leaves court to travel and seek his fortune. He has many adventures in remote places and undergoes trials from which he learns. (Orlando in the forest learns from his 'trials of love' by Rosalind.)

- Love and faithfulness: he loves a beautiful woman. She occupies all his thoughts. Constancy (fidelity) is highly valued. (Orlando falls instantly in love with Rosalind, and she with him.)
- Coincidence: all kinds of improbabilities and coincidences occur. (Anne Barton comments: 'The conclusion of *As You Like It* veers towards the implausible in asking us to accept four marriages, two lightning conversions, and the inexplicable appearance of the god Hymen'.)
- Fathers: a beautiful woman has a harsh father (Celia and Duke Frederick).
- Disguise: mistaken identity and disguise feature in many stories. (Rosalind disguises herself as a boy, Celia as a shepherdess. Neither is recognised.)
- Happy endings: the Knight marries his beloved, and the stories end with forgiveness, reconciliations, and virtue triumphant. (The play ends in multiple marriages, the reconciliation of Orlando and Oliver, the restoration of Duke Senior, and the conversion from evil of Duke Frederick.)

Many members of Shakespeare's audience came to the Globe Theatre with a deep knowledge of pastoral romance literature. They expected to see its themes, characters and conventions portrayed onstage. Shakespeare fulfilled their expectations, but he also gave his audience something radically different. On the surface, Shakespeare seems to follow the tradition. The play is full of contrasts between court and country. The court is an unnatural and unhappy place. The country is natural and joyful. The court is corrupt and artificial, a world to escape from. The country is benign and delightful, a place of freedom.

Duke Senior declares the opposition between the two worlds in his first speech 'Are not these woods / More free from peril than the envious court?' Touchstone and Corin debate their contrasting views of court and country life. Amiens sings of the pleasures of life under the greenwood tree where there is 'No enemy / But winter and rough weather.' Another of his songs tells of 'man's ingratitude' and of false friendship ('Most friendship is feigning') in contrast to life under the green holly. In the court, brother is set against brother, and ambition, envy and intrigue are common. Duke Frederick has usurped his brother, and he exiles Rosalind on pain of death. In contrast, the exiles in Arden seem to live contentedly as a friendly community.

But Shakespeare's portrayal of the theme of town versus country is not a simple opposition of bad versus good. The Forest of Arden is not an idealised utopia. Its winds are biting, an 'icy fang'. The old carlot (peasant) who employs Corin is a hard taskmaster, Phebe cruelly scorns the besotted Silvius. The deer are hunted to death by the exiled lords, and snakes and lions threaten life. Duke Senior maintains the hierarchy of the court. Jaques cynically comments on the foolishness of the man who leaves 'his wealth and ease' for the rough pleasures of the forest. Audrey is quite unlike the idealised shepherdess of the romantic tradition. Rosalind and Orlando discover that even in the Forest of Arden the path of true love does not run smooth. At the end of the play the exiles prepare to return to court. They do not seem unhappy to be leaving the country behind them. Only Jaques, the cynic, prefers to stay behind, and his purpose is not the enjoyment of the innocent pleasures of rural life.

What was Shakespeare's England like?

This section begins with some brief examples of particular allusions, then provides more extended discussions of features of Elizabethan England that have importance for understanding the play as a whole.

There are all kinds of references to contemporary events or gossip. When Rosalind says she 'will weep for nothing, like Diana in the fountain' (Act 4 Scene 1, lines 122–3) Shakespeare may have had in mind the fountain set up in London's Cheapside showing Diana, Roman goddess of chastity, with water flowing from her breasts. Similarly, he has Touchstone refer obliquely to the death of the playwright Christopher Marlowe, killed in 1593 in a dispute over the 'reckoning' (the bill) in a Deptford tavern:

> When a man's verses cannot be understood . . . it strikes a man more dead than a great reckoning in a little room.
>
> *(Act 3 Scene 4, lines 8–10)*

Some members of Shakespeare's audience would hear Touchstone's lines echoing a well-known line of Marlowe's: 'Infinite riches in a little room'. Later they would recognise Marlowe as the 'dead shepherd' who coined the wise saying ('saw') '"Who ever loved that loved not at first sight?"' (Act 3 Scene 6, line 81).

It is also possible that Elizabethan audiences would see Jaques as a caricature of one of Shakespeare's contemporaries. Both Ben Jonson and John Marston, fellow playwrights, have been suggested as Shakespeare's model for the melancholy cynic. The best-known claim, however, is for Sir John Harington, Queen Elizabeth's godson, and a favourite at court, popular for his wit. Harington invented the water closet, a forerunner of the modern flush toilet, known to the Elizabethans as a privy. He wrote a book, *The Metamorphosis of Ajax*, describing his invention. 'Ajax' puns on 'jakes', a slang term for a privy. Jaques (pronounced 'jakes') is thought to be Shakespeare's in-joke, encouraging his audience to identify Jaques as Harington. It must be noted, however, that many critics reject the notion that Jaques, or any character, was Shakespeare's parody of an actual person. Their view that the character is based on a character type common in Elizabethan England is discussed on pages 72–4 and 121, but here it is helpful to consider a character who many find puzzling: Sir Oliver Martext.

When Sir Oliver Martext turns up in Act 3 Scene 4 in a failed attempt to marry Touchstone and Audrey, many in Shakespeare's audience would recognise him as representing a familiar Elizabethan rural priest. Their ignorance and lack of learning had been roundly condemned in a 1586 survey of clergymen. For example, many in Warwickshire, Shakespeare's own county, had been judged 'incompetent . . . dumbe and unlearned'.

On hearing such matters of familiar knowledge, the response of Shakespeare's original audiences could work at different levels. For example, the more literary members of the audience would probably also see Martext as yet another of Shakespeare's contrasts of 'court versus country' (see pages 64–5). That knowledge would add to their enjoyment as they watched the sophisticated court characters Jaques and Touchstone ridicule the hapless country priest. Similarly, Elizabethan aristocrats would recognise, in Touchstone's 'we quarrel in print, by the book' (Act 5 Scene 4, line 78), that Shakespeare is satirising the many books on etiquette that were popular among upper-class men as guides to how courtiers should behave.

Many other aspects of everyday life in the Elizabethan world are quietly incorporated into the play. Silvius' description of the hangman asking pardon of the man he is about to execute (Act 3 Scene 6, lines 3–6) echoes just what contemporary executioners did. Rosalind's declaration that love is a madness, and 'deserves as well a dark-house and a whip', acknowledges a cruel 'cure' of the times. The mentally ill were thought to be possessed by devils, and were labelled as mad, locked in a dark room, and whipped to drive out the devils. Shakespeare staged this treatment in *Twelfth Night*, when Malvolio is called mad and locked in a dark room.

Similarly, when Jaques taunts Orlando that he has learned ('conned') his 'pretty answers' out of rings, and Orlando retorts that Jaques has learned ('studied') his questions from 'painted cloth' (Act 3 Scene 3, lines 230–3), their images rely on knowledge familiar to Elizabethans but virtually unknown today. Jaques implies that Orlando's answers come from the sentimental inscriptions that goldsmiths engraved inside rings. In return, Orlando implies that Jaques spends his time in tavern bedrooms. These were hung with cheap imitation tapestries ('painted cloth') with similar commonplace sayings painted on them.

Such examples show how Shakespeare's England provides a rich source for the imagery of the play. In particular, the Elizabethan interest in theatre, hunting, country life, field sports and animals is richly evident. You can find a more extended discussion of imagery on pages 76–9 and 90. Here it is sufficient to mention only such examples as Jaques' 'All the world's a stage', and how the hunters' song ('The horn, the horn, the lusty horn') and Touchstone's 'old cuckoldly ram' reveal the Elizabethans' obsession with horns and love of jokes about cuckolds: deceived husbands who were derided as having horns on their head.

The educated members of Shakespeare's audience would especially like the play for its many literary, biblical and classical allusions. They immediately understood Duke Senior's mention of 'discord in the spheres' (see page 21), and they recognised in the play the influence of the books they read for pleasure, picking up its references to the Roman poet Ovid, and the various elements of classical mythology (see page 78). They enjoyed how Shakespeare presented one of the hot topics of the day among the educated elite: whether poetry was true and sincere, or simply pretence and 'feigning'. When they heard that argument put into the mouths of a clown and a goatherd, Touchstone and Audrey, those audience members saw the debate being given a novel twist by their favourite playwright.

In addition to the topical reminders of everyday life described above there are other ways in which *As You Like It* reveals what Elizabethan England was like. What follows identifies important social and cultural contexts that influenced the creation of *As You Like It*.

Politics and protest

The theatre director Stephen Unwin comments on the sombre social context which he claims affected the response of Elizabethan audiences to *As You Like It*:

> Elizabeth's court by the end of the sixteenth century was increasingly adopting Duke Frederick's style of arbitrary and personalised decision-making. Profound questions were being asked about the legitimacy of the monarch's power, as well as about the new kind of thuggish profiteering personified by Orlando's older brother Oliver. Thus the many angry comments by Rosalind, Orlando, Adam and others about the 'fashion of these times', as well as Jaques' desire to 'cleanse the foul body of the infected world', must have held an extraordinary power over an audience caught up in a whirlwind of change, social disintegration and ultimately Civil war.

Unwin's analyis is typical of those critics who argue that Shakespeare's audience saw in *As You Like It* criticism of aspects of the society of their times. The most widely held view is that it portrays the injustices brought about in the English countryside through enclosures: the process by which landowners enriched themselves at the expense of the poor by enlarging their estates, taking over common land or the small plots previously worked by people living at, or only just above, subsistence level.

The argument is powerfully expressed by Richard Wilson, who sets the play in the context of the riots against enclosures and famines in the 1590s. Wilson sees *As You Like It* as 'a drama of enclosure and exclusion', and argues that Oliver represents 'the Elizabethan success story of the rise of the gentry by engrossing and enclosing at the expense of evicted relatives and tenants'. Wilson's view of *As You Like It* is that

No Shakespearean text transmits more urgently the imminence of the social breakdown threatened by the conjuncture of famine and enclosure.

Wilson claims that Shakespeare 'dramatised agrarian conflict in *As You Like It*', and argues that 'the play is powerfully inflected by narratives of popular resistance, whilst its plot . . . is the brutal story of Elizabethan social transformation'. Wilson's reading of the play sets it in the context of the many contemporary violent protests against enclosure. He produces evidence to show that the forests of England (including Warwickshire's own Forest of Arden) were places which housed many of those who suffered from the actions of enclosing landlords. They lived in communities outside the law, poaching the deer and sometimes taking violent measures against enclosure. Wilson asserts that the actual forest is a hotbed of sedition and potential rebellion.

Wilson interprets features of the play to show that it is aware 'that it is playing symbolically with fire' in presenting aspects of the conflict in the countryside. The play parades all the felonies associated with forest rioters: trespass, poaching, damaging trees, sending letters in fictitious names, and cross-dressing. *As You Like It*'s interest in disguise reflects how the rioters sometimes dressed as women to carry out night attacks to obstruct enclosures. The hunters of Act 4 Scene 2 represent rough music against enclosures, and edge 'closest to those rites of misrule' of the forest-dwelling rioters. Wilson sees Orlando as a kind of noble robber who upholds the collective values of the poor against the 'ambition' of the rich. His claim that he is 'inland bred' is seen as affiliating him with the Midland rioters who caused many problems for the authorities in Warwickshire. But Wilson argues that the play shows Orlando eventually supporting the old inegalitarian order that dominates the play.

Younger sons: primogeniture

One way of looking at *As You Like It* is to see it as a dramatisation of the plight of younger sons in Elizabethan England. In aristocratic families, by the custom of primogeniture the oldest son inherited all his father's wealth. The younger sons were therefore virtually wholly dependent on their older brother's generosity and goodwill. Orlando finds that Oliver does not possess such qualities. His father had left the bulk of his estate to Oliver with the injunction that he cares for and educates Orlando to the condition of a gentleman. But Oliver does quite the opposite in denying all privileges to Orlando, so evoking his complaint 'His horses are bred better.'

A real-life Elizabethan Orlando would indeed suffer financial and status handicaps. But Shakespeare uses the pastoral romance tradition and the Forest of Arden to remedy Orlando's situation. Among the forest outlaws he gains status, and through his marriage to Rosalind he becomes the heir to all the wealth and power of a duke. Reflecting on this, the critic Louis Montrose comments:

> In the world of its Elizabethan audience, the form of Orlando's experience may indeed have functioned as a collective compensation, a projection for the wish-fulfilment fantasies of younger brothers, youths, and all who felt themselves deprived by their fathers or their fortunes.

Women and patriarchy

In Elizabethan England, men were firmly in control. Husbands and fathers had virtually absolute authority over the lives of their wives and daughters. Women's status and roles were subject to the tyranny of patriarchy (rule by men). Their rights were restricted, legally, socially and economically. On marriage, all a woman's possessions passed to her husband. Religion was a powerful instrument to enforce the belief and practice of male superiority. The Elizabethan *Homily on the State of Matrimony* was frequently read aloud in church. It ordered wives to obey their husbands, and instructed husbands that 'the woman is a frail vessel and thou art therefore made the ruler and head over her'.

But *As You Like It* shows two women, Rosalind and Celia, who seem to enjoy a great deal of independence. Duke Frederick behaves like a stern Elizabethan father, expecting his daughter's instant obedience, forbidding her to plead against Rosalind's banishment ('Thou art a fool . . . open not thy lips!'). But Celia defies her father. She throws in her lot with Rosalind and takes the lead in persuading her to go to the Forest of Arden. In the forest the two women enjoy economic freedom, managing their own affairs. Rosalind takes the leading role in 'curing' Orlando, and in arranging the weddings at the play's end.

Rosalind's independent spirit reflects a different aspect of Elizabethan society. Whilst most women had little or no power or autonomy, some successfully did achieve independence, managing their own estates or business. Many ran their own households with little or no interference from their husbands. The stereotype of all Elizabethan males as patriarchal tyrants is far from the truth; in many families male–female relationships were based on equality of respect and love.

Nonetheless, the legal and economic condition of Elizabethan women is reflected at the play's end as all four female characters marry. All four will become subordinate to their husbands. Rosalind's words to Orlando and to her father acknowledge, even within the happiness of the ending of a delightful comedy, the harsh reality of male–female relationships in Shakespeare's England. Like any Elizabethan married woman, she becomes a possession of a man:

> To you I give myself, for I am yours.
>
> *(Act 5 Scene 4, lines 101–2)*

You can find discussion of other aspects of gender in the Feminist criticism section on pages 97–100.

Religion

Elizabethan England was a profoundly religious society. Virtually everybody in the land cared passionately about religion. It pervaded almost every aspect of life. The English language was permeated with the language of religion. It is not surprising, therefore, that religious references abound in *As You Like It*. Some are brief, but symbolically important, such as Rosalind's mention of Ganymede's 'old religious uncle', or the report of the 'old religious man' who converted Duke Frederick. On his first appearance Jaques expresses the wish to 'rail against all the first-born of Egypt', invoking biblical knowledge of the plague God visited on Egypt's children. As he waits for the various couples to marry, and watches Touchstone and Audrey enter, Jaques sardonically remarks, 'There is sure another flood toward, and these couples are coming to the ark' (Act 5 Scene 4, lines 35–6). His image evokes the biblical story of Noah's ark, in which pairs of animals survived the Flood.

Other lines directly echo passages from the Bible. As Adam hands over all his savings to Orlando, he prays 'He that doth the ravens feed, / Yea providently caters for the sparrow, / Be comfort to my age' (Act 2 Scene 3, lines 43–5). The pagan god Hymen's song has New Testament resonances: 'Then is there mirth in heaven, / When earthly things made even / Atone together' (Act 5 Scene 4, lines 93–5).

Some members of an Elizabethan audience may have been shocked to see Celia acting as a priest to carry out a mock marriage of Orlando and Rosalind (women were strictly forbidden any such role). But all audience members would have recognised echoes of a church litany in the vocabulary, rhythm and meanings of the exchange between Orlando and Duke Senior: 'If ever you have looked on better days . . . That to your wanting may be ministered'(Act 2 Scene 7, lines 113–26). It embodies the Christian ideals of pity, gentleness, humility and loving-kindness that were familiar to Elizabethans from what they heard in church every Sunday and what they read in the New Testament of the Bible:

ORLANDO   If ever you have looked on better days,
    If ever been where bells have knolled to church,
    If ever sat at any goodman's feast,
    If ever from your eyelids wiped a tear,
    And know what 'tis to pity and be pitied,
    Let gentleness my strong enforcement be,
    In the which hope, I blush, and hide my sword.
DUKE SENIOR   True is it that we have seen better days,
    And have with holy bell been knolled to church,
    And sat at goodmen's feasts, and wiped our eyes
    Of drops that sacred pity hath engendered:
    And therefore sit you down in gentleness
    And take upon command what help we have
    That to your wanting may be ministered.

(Act 2 Scene 7, lines 113–26)

The melancholy man: the malcontent

Today, 'melancholy' usually means sad, depressed or morosely introverted. But it included other meanings in Shakespeare's time: serious, cynical, world-weary. Elizabethans were fascinated by what we now call neuroses or 'complexes'. They used the theory of the four humours to explain people's behaviour, personalities or moods. A popular belief was that personality was determined by four 'humours' (fluids in the human body). These were blood (producing bravery), phlegm (producing calmness), 'yellowe bile' (producing anger), and black bile (producing melancholy). The belief was that if the four humours were in balance, the result was a healthy and temperate person. But if one humour dominated, the outcome was an unbalanced personality. Many Elizabethans would think that Jaques, with his extreme melancholy, had an excess of black bile.

Playwrights frequently put characters onstage who displayed extremes of behaviour (jealousy, anger, sadness, etc.), and Jaques is perhaps the most famous stage depiction of 'the melancholy man'. He seems to delight in his melancholy. In his conversation with Rosalind in Act 4 Scene 1 he takes great care to fashion his image, claiming that his personality is quite different from anyone else's. But it is a melancholy pose that many Elizabethan gentlemen affected: the world-weary cynic who feels that he has seen it all, and his travels have made him an aloof commentator on human folly.

Jaques is also often seen as an example of the malcontent, a familiar figure of the times, both in real life and in theatre. The malcontent is a character type in Elizabethan and Jacobean drama. He is like 'the angry young man' of the 1960s: a discontented or melancholy man, who rails bitterly at the society in which he lives. The malcontent reflected the fashionable pose that many courtiers adopted in Shakespeare's time. Such a man would express dissatisfaction with himself and with everything around him: family, state, nature itself. Unhappy, and critical of everything and everybody, the malcontent was socially and psychologically dislocated.

Different kinds of malcontent appear in Shakespeare's plays. They appear in all kinds of guises. In *Troilus and Cressida*, Thersites is an extreme example, as is the misanthropic (humankind-hating) Timon of Athens; both are bitterly fierce critics of humanity. In the tragedies, characters playing the malcontent role include such diverse individuals as the evil villains Iago in *Othello*, Edmund in *King Lear* and Aaron in *Titus Andronicus*. Even the deeply introspective Prince Hamlet can be seen as a malcontent, unhappy and dispossessed of his right to succeed his father. So too is the cynical Cassius in *Julius Caesar*, and the blunt soldier Enobarbus in *Antony and Cleopatra*, who is critical of Antony's folly, and finally disgusted with himself.

The critic Agnes Latham identifies the Elizabethans' intense interest in melancholy, the 'humour' that expressed itself in a detached, contemplative and sceptical view of the world. She sees Jaques as representative of that humour, but warns against interpreting him as a stereotypical malcontent. Rather, he enjoys his melancholy, and never appears depressed:

> He is entirely free of the malcontent's sense of personal injury.
> He never suggests that the world has treated him more
> unfairly than anyone else. He proposes to 'cleanse' it, but not
> to pay scores. His banishment seems to have been voluntarily
> undertaken, and he certainly elects to prolong it voluntarily.

The Fool

Fools were often employed in the palaces of royalty or great houses of noble families. Although they had the title of 'fool' (or jester or clown), they were much more intelligent than foolish. Their job was not simply to provide amusement, by singing, dancing and joking, but also to make critical comment on contemporary behaviour. An 'allowed fool' was able to say what he thought, and had licence to criticise the follies of his master or other high-status persons. No punishment would follow.

Touchstone is such a licensed fool. He is employed by Duke Frederick and seems very much his own man, an observer and a sceptic. But in the court of Frederick his licence is limited. When he makes a comment critical of the Duke, Celia sharply reminds him of the punishment that is likely to follow:

> Enough! Speak no more of him; you'll be whipped for
> taxation one of these days.   *(Act 1 Scene 2, lines 66–7)*

In *Shakespeare the Craftsman* Muriel Bradbrook sets Touchstone in the context of the stage fools of Elizabethan and Jacobean times. In particular, she identifies the actors who played such roles in Shakespeare's own acting company. Throughout the 1590s the company's leading clown was Will Kempe. He played the comic roles of Peter in *Romeo and Juliet* and Dogberry in *Much Ado About Nothing*. When Kempe left the company in 1599 his place was taken by Robert Armin. Bradbrook argues that Armin's distinctive qualities led

Shakespeare to create Touchstone (and such other roles as Feste in *Twelfth Night*, the Gravedigger in *Hamlet*, and the Fool in *King Lear*):

> The new feature about these parts is that they are dramatically interwoven with the central characters and the central feelings of a play; they demand an actor to play many parts, not just his own brand of clowning.

Bradbrook notes that Armin's comic roles share common characteristics: he attends upon ladies (Celia and Rosalind), he enjoys proving others fools (Corin and William), he is given to music and song (mocking Sir Oliver Martext), and possesses a deflating wit. Bradbrook argues that the way in which Touchstone questions Rosalind and Celia in Act 1, and his catechising (questioning) of Corin in Act 3 Scene 3 is typical of Armin's comic style.

Shakespeare's own life

This section began with the film *Shakespeare in Love*. It is a delightful fantasy which gives the impression that the inspiration for *Romeo and Juliet* was Shakespeare's own personal experience of falling in love. Today, critics and examiners give little or no credit to approaches which interpret *As You Like It* in the context of Shakespeare's emotional life, because nothing is really known of his intimate thoughts, feelings or activities. Today the focus of critical attention is on social and cultural contexts such as those identified in this section.

An important critical question about those contexts concerns Shakespeare's attitude to them: what was his personal view of the practices, conventions and values of the time? What was his attitude to love, or to melancholy? Is the play a subtle and ironic critique of male power, showing that even such a spirited, independent and capable female as Rosalind finally accepts male dominance? Once again, no one really knows for certain. But as this section shows, what is clear is that *As You Like It* is richly influenced by many features of Shakespeare's England. And as the Critical approaches section (pages 86–106) shows, it is possible to construct persuasive arguments to support very different interpretations of the attitude of the play (or Shakespeare) to the various contextual features and issues that the play dramatises.

Language

Ben Jonson famously remarked that Shakespeare 'wanted art' (lacked technical skill). But Jonson's comment is mistaken, as is the popular image of Shakespeare as a 'natural' writer, utterly spontaneous, inspired only by his imagination. Shakespeare possessed a profound knowledge of the language techniques of his own and previous times. Behind the apparent effortlessness of the language lies a deeply practised skill. That skill is evident in *As You Like It* in all kinds of ways, for, as Brian Vickers notes:

> no other play contains as many witty set speeches . . . in no other play are logic and rhetoric used so brilliantly . . .
> Touchstone and Rosalind produce the most brilliant display of witty prose in the canon.

What follows are some of the language techniques Shakespeare uses in *As You Like It* to intensify dramatic effect, create mood and character, and so produce memorable theatre. The techniques are found in prose and verse alike. As you read them, always keep in mind that Shakespeare wrote for the stage, and that actors will therefore employ a wide variety of both verbal and non-verbal methods to exploit the dramatic possibilities of the language. They will use the full range of their voices and accompany the words with appropriate expressions, gestures and actions.

Imagery

As You Like It abounds in imagery (sometimes called 'figures' or 'figurative language'): vivid words and phrases that help create the atmosphere of the play as they conjure up emotionally-charged mental pictures in the imagination. When the disguised Rosalind tells Orlando that she lives 'here in the skirts of the forest, like fringe upon a petticoat' the femininity of her image almost gives away her disguise. She quickly recovers, however, and claims she is as native to the forest 'As the cony' (rabbit). When she tells Celia that the depth of her love for Orlando is bottomless 'like the Bay of Portugal', the intensity of her feelings is vividly conveyed in the image.

Shakespeare seems to have thought in images, and the whole play richly demonstrates his unflagging and varied use of verbal illustration. Perhaps the best-known example is Jaques' 'seven ages of man' speech with its imaginative portrayals of the infant crying and vomiting ('Mewling and puking') in the nurse's arms, the miserable schoolboy 'creeping like snail / Unwillingly to school' and so on. Celia uses an image from bricklaying to suggest that Touchstone is thickly laying on the irony in his imitation of Le Beau: 'that was laid on with a trowel.' Rosalind delivers a long set piece on Time as an ambling, trotting, galloping or immobile horse, and uses engaged girls, priests, thieves and lawyers as illustrations (Act 3 Scene 3, lines 261–80). And she uses extravagant imagery to express her suspense as Celia postpones telling her news of Orlando:

> I would thou couldst stammer that thou mightst pour this
> concealed man out of thy mouth as wine comes out of a
> narrow-mouthed bottle: either too much at once or none at all.
> I prithee take the cork out of thy mouth that I may drink thy
> tidings.
>
> *(Act 3 Scene 3, lines 165–9)*

Early critics such as John Dryden and Doctor Johnson were critical of Shakespeare's fondness for imagery. They felt that many images obscured meaning and detracted attention from the subjects they represented. Over the past 200 years, however, critics, poets and audiences have increasingly valued Shakespeare's imagery. They recognise how he uses it to help create the play's distinctive atmosphere and themes, and to give pleasure as it stirs the audience's imagination, deepens the dramatic impact of particular moments or moods, provides insight into character, and intensifies meaning and emotional force. Images carry powerful significance far deeper than their surface meanings.

As noted in the Contexts section of this Guide, Shakespeare's Elizabethan world provides much of the play's imagery. The world is imagined as a stage, Rosalind's cares as briars and burrs, Phebe's occasional smiles on Silvius as the broken ears of corn left over in a harvest field. Celia describes Orlando as hollow as a goblet or a worm-eaten nut, and Rosalind imagines him like a dropped acorn. But in *As You Like It* Shakespeare also gently mocks the use of imagery. In Act

3 Scene 6, lines 8–27 he gives Phebe 20 lines in which she ridicules the image that a lover's eyes can wound.

Shakespeare's imagery uses simile, metaphor or personification. All are comparisons which in effect substitute one thing (the image) for another (the thing described):

- A simile compares one thing to another using 'like' or 'as'. The exiled court is described as living in the Forest of Arden 'like the old Robin Hood of England'; Celia laughs with Rosalind that Le Beau will cram them with news 'as pigeons feed their young'; Adam declares his 'age is as a lusty winter'; Jaques pictures the schoolboy 'creeping like snail / Unwillingly to school'; and Rosalind complains that listening to Silvius, Phebe and Orlando echoing each other's declarations of love is 'like the howling of Irish wolves against the moon'.

- A metaphor is also a comparison. It does not use 'like' or 'as' but suggests that two dissimilar things are actually the same. Examples are Rosalind labelling Silvius 'a tame snake', Orlando calling himself 'a rotten tree', and Touchstone insulting Corin as 'worms' meat'. To put it another way, a metaphor borrows one word or phrase to express another. For example, when Rosalind says that 'men are April when they woo, December when they wed' her image wittily but bitterly expresses the passionate nature ('April') of a man's courtship, and its dwindling into cold indifference ('December') after marriage.

- Personification turns all kinds of things or ideas into persons, giving them human feelings or attributes: 'the good housewife Fortune', 'the swift foot of Time'. Jaques and Orlando use personification to bid each other a mocking farewell as 'Signor Love' and 'Monsieur Melancholy'.

Classical mythology contributes to the richness of the play's imagery. Hymen, the Greek and Roman god of marriage, appears as a character, and there are mentions of Hercules, Cupid, Jupiter, Juno, Diana, Venus and other mythical figures. Elizabethans were usually more familiar with the symbolism of such references than are most members of audiences today. Celia describes how she and Rosalind have been inseparable 'like Juno's swans' who drew the chariot of the queen of the gods. Orlando's praise of Rosalind (Act 3 Scene 3, lines

120–3) compares her with famous women in Greek and Roman mythology or history.

Rosalind's choice of Ganymede carried both classical and popular significance for Elizabethans. In Greek mythology Ganymede was a beautiful young man. Jupiter (Jove), king of the gods, fell in love with him, and, disguised as an eagle, carried him off to Mount Olympus to become his cup-bearer (page). But Ganymede was also Elizabethan slang for a young male homosexual.

Antithesis

Antithesis is the opposition of words or phrases against each other, as when Celia sets 'liberty' against 'banishment' in declaring that she and Rosalind will go to the Forest of Arden 'To liberty, and not to banishment.' Similarly antithetical is Duke Frederick's angry remark to Orlando:

> The world esteemed thy father honourable
> But I did find him still mine enemy.
>
> *(Act 1 Scene 2, lines 177–8)*

This setting of word against word ('world' opposes 'I', and 'honourable' contrasts with 'enemy') is one of Shakespeare's favourite language devices. He uses it extensively in all his plays. Why? Because antithesis powerfully expresses and intensifies conflict through its use of opposites, and conflict is the essence of all drama. Shakespeare's dramatic style is characterised by his concern for comparison and contrast, opposition and juxtaposition: he sets character against character, scene against scene, emotional tone against emotional tone, word against word, phrase against phrase.

Although *As You Like It* is a comedy, it is full of conflict: brother versus brother, court versus country, appearance against reality (most notably in Rosalind's disguise as a male), and the conflicts of love itself. The critic Helen Gardner provides a reminder that in the play

> points of view put forward by one character find contradiction or correction by another, so that the whole play is a balance of sweet against sour, of the cynical against the idealistic, and life is shown as a mingling of hard fortune and good hap . . . It is a play of meetings and encounters, of conversations and sets of

wit: Orlando versus Jaques, Touchstone versus Corin, Rosalind versus Jaques, Rosalind versus Phebe, and above all Rosalind versus Orlando.

Each feature of the play that Gardner mentions contains antitheses in the dialogue. And it is valuable to note that one of the play's dominant themes, court versus country (see pages 64–5) is made explicit in the antitheses throughout Duke Senior's first speech, as he opposes life in Arden to that in the court. It begins:

> Hath not old custom made this life more sweet
> Than that of painted pomp? Are not these woods
> More free from peril than the envious court?
>
> *(Act 2 Scene 1, lines 2–4)*

Repetition

Different forms of language repetitions run through the play, contributing to its atmosphere, creation of character and dramatic force. Apart from familiar functional words ('the', 'and', etc.) the lexical word most frequently repeated is 'love' (used over 110 times). Its repetition is a clear indication of the major preoccupation of the play.

Shakespeare's skill in using repetition to heighten theatrical effect and deepen emotional and imaginative significance is most evident in particular speeches. Repeated words ('O Phebe, Phebe, Phebe!'), phrases, rhythms and sounds add humour or intensity to the moment or episode. Both the verse and prose of the play contain similar qualities of rhythmical and phrase repetition. Some episodes have an almost ritualistic quality because particular phrases and rhythms are repeated:

- Silvius' first appearance, with his refrain 'thou hast not loved' (Act 2 Scene 4, lines 27–36);
- the echoing exchange between Orlando and Duke Senior: 'If ever you have looked on better days' (Act 2 Scene 7, lines 113–26);
- the three lovers who repeat Silvius' litany of love: 'And so am I for Phebe.' (Act 5 Scene 2, lines 67–90);
- Rosalind's promise to satisfy the wishes of each lover: 'I will help you, if I can.' (Act 5 Scene 2, lines 92–100).

Repetition also occasionally occurs in rhyme (repeated sounds). It is most obvious in each of the songs, in Orlando's doggerel poems (Act 3 Scene 3), Phebe's letter (Act 4 Scene 3), and in the couplets which end some scenes, for example in Duke Senior's final words:

> Proceed, proceed. – We will begin these rites
> As we do trust they'll end, in true delights.
>
> *(Act 5 Scene 4, lines 181–2)*

Lists

One of Shakespeare's favourite language methods is to accumulate words or phrases rather like a list. He had learned the technique as a schoolboy in Stratford-upon-Avon, and his skill in knowing how to use lists dramatically is evident in *As You Like It*. The most famous example is Jaques' 'seven ages of man' speech, and there are many other lists in the play. Shakespeare intensifies and varies description, atmosphere and argument as he 'piles up' item on item, incident on incident. The accumulating effect of lists can amplify meaning and provide extra dimensions of character.

Sometimes the list comprises only single words or phrases, as in Rosalind's description of all the things she did when she pretended to be an inconstant mistress to cure a man of love: 'grieve, be effeminate, changeable, longing and liking, proud, fantastical, apish, shallow, inconstant, full of tears, full of smiles' (Act 3 Scene 3, lines 338–40). Altogether Rosalind lists 18 ways in which she 'cured' the lover (lines 336–46), and other lists, like the following, are similarly extended:

- Corin's list of his contentments (Act 3 Scene 3, lines 53–6);
- Rosalind's breathless list of questions about Orlando: 'What did he . . .?' (Act 3 Scene 3, lines 185–8);
- the ten 'marks' of a man in love: 'A lean cheek . . .' (Act 3 Scene 3, lines 312–8);
- Jaques' description of different kinds of melancholy (Act 4 Scene 1, lines 9–16);
- Touchstone's threats to William (Act 5 Scene 1, lines 41–50);
- Silvius' list of what it is to love (Act 5 Scene 2, lines 67–81);
- Touchstone's twice-repeated catalogue of how to avoid a duel: 'I will name you the degrees' (Act 5 Scene 4, lines 79–83).

All these lists richly display the features mentioned above: imagery, antithesis and repetition (as you can see in the example given in the following 'Prose' section). The many lists in the play provide valuable opportunities for actors to vary their delivery. In speaking, a character usually seeks to give each 'item' a distinctiveness in emphasis and emotional tone, and sometimes an accompanying action and expression.

Prose

Over half of *As You Like It* is in prose: almost 1,300 lines against just over 1,100 lines of verse. How did Shakespeare decide whether to write in verse or prose? One answer is that he followed theatrical convention. Prose was traditionally used by comic and low-status characters. High-status characters spoke verse. 'Comic' scenes were written in prose (as were letters), but audiences expected verse in 'serious' scenes: the poetic style was thought to be particularly suitable for lovers and for moments of high dramatic or emotional intensity. So prose was felt suitable to comedy, verse to tragedy and to history plays.

The high frequency of prose strongly suggests that Shakespeare saw *As You Like It* primarily as a comedy. But he used his judgement about which conventions or principles he should follow, and the play shows that he increasingly broke the 'rules'. In earlier comedies (*The Comedy of Errors, The Two Gentlemen of Verona, A Midsummer Night's Dream*) his upper-class characters, although 'comic', usually speak in verse.

But in *As You Like It* Rosalind and Celia (both princesses) and Orlando (also high status) use both verse and prose. Duke Frederick (high status) uses prose on his first appearance. But Silvius and Phebe, the shepherd and shepherdess (low status), speak in verse, and Adam (low status) uses both prose and verse. It may be that as he wrote *As You Like It* Shakespeare used prose or verse depending on whether he felt the situation to be 'comic' or 'serious'. But even that explanation is questionable: Oliver uses prose as he urges Charles the wrestler to harm Orlando (a 'serious' episode).

It seems likely that an Elizabethan audience was much more likely than a modern one to 'hear' the difference between verse and prose spoken onstage, and to respond differently to each. So Shakespeare may have switched between prose and verse as part of his dramatic construction, hoping to achieve different effects upon his audience. For example, the first half of the wrestling scene (Act 1 Scene 2) is in prose, but it switches to verse at the moment Duke Frederick discovers Orlando is the son of his enemy.

It is important to remember that although prose is less formally or obviously patterned than verse, Shakespeare's prose is nonetheless patterned, and usually possesses, in looser form, the symmetrical features found in verse: rhythm, repetition, imagery, antithesis, lists and balanced phrases and sentences. Within speeches and dialogue, sentences or phrases frequently balance, reflect or oppose each other. A typical example is Touchstone's reply to Corin's question 'And how like you this shepherd's life . . .?' His response is a list of paired, symmetrical antitheses expressed in repeated phrases:

> Truly, shepherd, in respect of itself, it is a good life; but in respect that it is a shepherd's life, it is naught. In respect that it is solitary, I like it very well; but in respect that it is private, it is a very vile life. Now in respect it is in the fields, it pleaseth me well; but in respect it is not in the court, it is tedious. As it is a spare life, look you, it fits my humour well; but as there is no more plenty in it, it goes much against my stomach.
>
> (Act 3 Scene 3, lines 2–8)

Verse

The verse of *As You Like It* is mainly blank verse: unrhymed verse written in iambic pentameter. It is conventional to define iambic pentameter as a rhythm or metre in which each line has five stressed syllables (/) alternating with five unstressed syllables (×) as when Rosalind describes her height:

×　/　×　/×　　/　　×　/　　×　/
Because that I am more than common tall

At school, Shakespeare had learned the technical definition of iambic pentameter. In Greek *penta* means 'five', and *iamb* means a 'foot' of two syllables, the first unstressed, the second stressed, as in 'alas' = aLAS. Shakespeare practised writing in that metre, and his early plays, such as *Titus Andronicus* or *Richard III* are very regular in rhythm (expressed as de-DUM de-DUM de-DUM de-DUM de-DUM), and with each ten-syllable line 'end-stopped' (making sense on its own).

By the time he came to write *As You Like It* (around 1599–1600), Shakespeare had become more flexible and experimental in his use of iambic pentameter. The 'five-beat' rhythm is still present, but is less prominent. End-stopped lines are less frequent. There is greater use of *enjambement* (running on), where one line flows on into the next, seemingly with little or no pause, as in Oliver's story of the threats to his life in Act 4 Scene 3, lines 101–8:

> A wretched ragged man, o'ergrown with hair,
> Lay sleeping on his back; about his neck
> A green and gilded snake had wreathed itself,
> Who, with her head, nimble in threats, approached
> The opening of his mouth. But suddenly
> Seeing Orlando, it unlinked itself
> And with indented glides did slip away
> Into a bush

The songs, Orlando's poems, Phebe's letter and Hymen's blessings are all in verse, but not in the five-beat rhythm of iambic pentameter. Some critics, directors and actors have strong convictions about how the verse should be spoken. For example, the director Peter Hall insists there should always be a pause at the end of each line. But it seems appropriate when studying (or watching or acting in) *As You Like It*, not to attempt to apply rigid rules about verse speaking. Shakespeare certainly used the convention of iambic pentameter, but he did not adhere to it slavishly. He knew 'the rules', but he was not afraid to break them to suit his dramatic purposes. And perhaps he was laughing at actors who spoke iambic pentameter in a clockwork rhythm when he has Jaques respond testily to a ten-syllable line of Orlando's:

ORLANDO   Good day, and happiness, dear Rosalind.
JAQUES   Nay then, God buy you, and you talk in blank verse!

(Act 4 Scene 1, lines 24–5)

Songs

There are seven songs in the play:

- 'Under the greenwood tree' and Jaques' parody of it, 'If it do come to pass' (Act 2 Scene 5)
- 'Blow, blow, thou winter wind' (Act 2 Scene 7)
- 'O sweet Oliver' (Act 3 Scene 4)
- 'What shall he have that killed the deer?' (Act 4 Scene 2)
- 'It was a lover and his lass' (Act 5 Scene 3)
- 'Wedding is great Juno's crown' (Act 5 Scene 4)

The songs may be Shakespeare's response to the popularity of the children's acting companies of the time, whose singing attracted large audiences. Or perhaps there was a gifted singer in Shakespeare's own acting company, so Shakespeare inserted the songs specially for him. Or maybe Shakespeare thought the songs were particularly suited to the pastoral mood of the play – or he simply wanted the audience to enjoy his songs!

Puns and wordplay

Shakespeare and his contemporaries loved wordplay of all kinds: 'How now, wit, whither wander you?' Puns were especially popular. A pun is a play on words where the same sound or word has different meanings. Finding himself in the Forest of Arden, Touchstone puns on 'bear' and 'cross' and, in his tale of Jane Smile, and in his meeting with Jaques, on words which had sexual meanings for Elizabethans. (Act 2 Scenes 4 and 7). Rosalind puns on 'hart' (female deer) when, hearing that Orlando is dressed like a hunter, she cries 'He comes to kill my heart.' The most intriguing wordplay is when Rosalind (disguised as Ganymede) persuades Orlando to woo her/him (Act 4 Scene 1, lines 31–176). Orlando thinks he is speaking to a boy, but Rosalind revels in the ambiguity that her disguise gives. She can speak as herself without Orlando knowing it: 'I do take thee, Orlando, for my husband.'

Critical approaches

Traditional criticism

The first known performance of the play took place in 1740, and for almost 200 years afterwards criticism of the play typically comprised generalised praise, discussion of plot and character, and identification of moral insights embodied in the pastoral setting or in such episodes as the 'seven ages of man' speech. For example, the leading eighteenth-century critic Doctor Samuel Johnson wrote:

> Of this play the fable is wild and pleasing. I know not how the ladies will approve the facility with which both Rosalind and Celia give away their hearts . . . The character of Jaques is natural and well preserved. The comic dialogue is very sprightly . . . and the graver part is elegant and harmonious.

Johnson is representative of the writing of his time which attempted to find moral instruction in the theatre. For example, he regretted that Shakespeare had not written a scene showing the meeting of Duke Frederick with the old religious man who persuaded him to give up his military expedition to destroy his brother Duke Senior. For Johnson, Shakespeare had 'lost an opportunity of exhibiting a moral lesson'. From the late eighteenth century, through the nineteenth, and well into the twentieth, that focus on moral judgement, particularly of characters as if they were real persons, continued in critical writing about *As You Like It*.

William Hazlitt's criticism illustrates the tradition. In his significantly titled *The Characters of Shakespeare's Plays* (1817), he benevolently judges Jaques 'the prince of philosophical idlers; his only passion is thought', and sees Rosalind's character 'made up of sportive gaiety and natural tenderness'. His comments on the Forest of Arden and Duke Senior's praise of life there exemplify how *As You Like It* provided the Romantics of the early nineteenth century with rich material in which to find moral lessons:

> The very air of the place seems to breathe a spirit of philosophical poetry; to stir the thoughts, to touch the heart

with pity, as the drowsy forest rustles to the sighing gale.
Never was there such beautiful moralising, equally free from
pedantry or petulance.

> And this our life exempt from public haunt
> Finds tongues in trees, books in the running brooks,
> Sermons in stones, and good in everything.
>
> *(Act 2 Scene 1, lines 15–17)*

Hazlitt expresses the Romantics' belief that society corrupts (both
actual society and the fictional court of Duke Frederick), and that
wisdom and goodness is to be found in nature. As will become clear
below, Hazlitt's benign view of Arden's 'sequestered and romantic
glades' has given way to harsher judgements of the forest.

A comment by the late nineteenth-century critic Edward Dowden
serves to illustrate another characteristic of traditional criticism:

> Jaques died, we know not how, or when, or where; but he
> came to life again a century later, and appeared in the world as
> an English clergyman; we need stand in no doubt as to his
> character, for we all know him under his later name of
> Laurence Sterne.

Dowden's discussion of Jaques as if he were a real person is
obvious. So too is the light-hearted tone as Dowden fancifully
imagines Jaques reincarnated as the popular eighteenth-century
author, whose writings (such as the novel *Tristram Shandy*, 1760)
humorously but critically examined the conventions of the times. But
it is Dowden's use of the first person plural ('we') that calls for
immediate comment. It is a style that has bedevilled critical writing
right up to the present time. Like all critics who use 'we', Dowden was
attempting to pass off his own knowledge and response as something
everybody feels (or should feel).

Such use of language is suspect, because many people simply do
not share the knowledge or sympathies expressed. It also condescends
and excludes: if you do not agree with Dowden's judgement you are
not 'one of us'. For example, it can equally plausibly be asserted that
Jaques would be a far more acerbic critic of human and social follies
than Laurence Sterne. As noted in the Organising your responses

section of this Guide, the use of 'we', 'our', etc. is best avoided in your own writing.

Hazlitt and Dowden display a typical tone of nineteenth-century criticism of *As You Like It* in its preoccupation with character. But the critic with whom the expression 'character study' is most associated is A C Bradley. Around 100 years ago, Bradley delivered a course of lectures at Oxford University which were published in 1904 as *Shakespearean Tragedy*, a book which is still in print and widely read.

Although Bradley makes only three very brief references to *As You Like It* (he is centrally concerned with *Hamlet, Macbeth, Othello, King Lear*), his form of criticism reflects previous approaches to the play, and has strongly influenced critical approaches right up to the present day. Bradley talks of the characters in Shakespeare as if they were real human beings experiencing familiar human emotions and thoughts, and existing in worlds recognisable to modern readers. He identifies the unique desires and motives which give characters their particular personalities, and which evoke feelings of admiration or disapproval in the audience.

Bradley's character approach has been much criticised, particularly for its neglect of the Elizabethan contexts of the plays' creation: the cultural and intellectual assumptions of the time, stage conditions, and poetic and dramatic conventions (pages 58–75 of this Guide demonstrate the powerful influence on *As You Like It* of such contexts). The most frequent objection to Bradley, however, is his treatment of characters as real people. Modern criticism is uneasy about discussing characters in this way, preferring to see them as fictional creations in a stage drama.

Although Bradley has fallen from critical favour, his influence is still evident. As page 122 shows, it is difficult to avoid talking or writing about characters as if they were living people and making moral judgements on them. But it would be inappropriate to think of traditional criticism as concerned solely with a Bradley-like approach to character. All kinds of different approaches exist within it. For example, some scholars have attempted to identify actual people on whom Shakespeare based his characters, most memorably the claim that Jaques caricatures Sir John Harington, inventor of the privy or 'jakes' (see page 66).

A more convincing strand of criticism concerns itself with an approach to character as embodying the themes of the play or representing 'types'. As Agnes Latham argues, 'It is more profitable to trace in Jaques the generic traits of the melancholy man than to suppose him a caricature of a particular person'. Her view of Jaques as an example of the malcontent, a familiar character type in Elizabethan literature and society, is discussed on pages 72–4.

Other different critical approaches are evident in Helen Gardner's 1959 essay 'Let the Forest Judge'. It ranges over such matters as sources, genre, Arden as a place of learning, the ways in which lies and feigning enable the discovery of truth, and how the play embodies the recurring Christian ideals of loving kindness, gentleness, pity and humility. Gardner notes how much the play owes to the folk tale and pastoral romance tradition. She argues that Shakespeare handles plot in a very perfunctory way, cramming the first act with incident to get everyone to the forest as quickly as possible, and ending the play with similar speed. Gardner is certain that Shakespeare was not concerned with story in *As You Like It*, and she looks for 'its soul' elsewhere. She sees Arden as a place where characters endlessly discuss, where Rosalind discovers the limits of her disguise as Ganymede, and where Phebe discovers that love is better than scorn. She concludes:

> This discovery of truth by feigning, and of what is wisdom and what folly by debate, is the centre of *As You Like It*.

But within Gardner's subtle discussion, the assumptions of traditional character criticism are evident: 'Whose society would you prefer, Le Beau's or Audrey's?'; 'William is a dolt and Audrey graceless'. But such 'real-person' judgements are tempered by an awareness of characters' dramatic functions and of their representativeness of types or humours:

> The two commentators of the play are nicely contrasted. Touchstone is the parodist, Jaques the cynic . . . The clown is never baffled and is marked by his ability to place himself at once *en rapport* with his audience, to be all things to all men, to perform the part which is required at the moment. Touchstone sustains many different roles . . . Jaques is his opposite. He is the cynic, the person who prefers the pleasures of superiority, cold-eyed and cold-hearted.

Caroline Spurgeon opened up a further critical perspective on *As You Like It*: the study of its imagery. In *Shakespeare's Imagery and What it Tells Us*, Spurgeon identifies patterns of imagery in each of Shakespeare's plays. She finds that *As You Like It* 'fairly scintillates with wit, largely in the form of images'. The conversations between Rosalind and Celia, and Rosalind and Orlando are 'a mass of verbal fireworks in metaphor and simile', and Jaques is 'one of the great simile makers in Shakespeare' (see page 78 for a discussion of metaphor and simile). Spurgeon remarks on the high number of nature images in the play, which help create its atmosphere of outdoor country life. She notes the similar effect of the many animal similes, more than in any other of Shakespeare's comedies:

> the doe going to find her fawn to give it food, the weasel sucking eggs, chanticleer crowing, the wild goose flying, pigeons feeding, and such vivid glimpses of animal passion and emotion as those given us by Rosalind 'there was never anything so sudden but the fight of two rams', 'I will be more jealous of thee than a Barbary cock-pigeon over his hen'.

Although the value of Caroline Spurgeon's pioneering study of Shakespeare's imagery has been acknowledged by later critics, her work has also been much criticised. For example, she only occasionally examines how the imagery relates to the dramatic context of the play, and makes no mention of sexual imagery. She claims that the imagery reveals Shakespeare's personal life ('We are constantly reminded of Shakespeare's favourite haunts of garden and orchard'), and her preference for praise rather than for any any critical appraisal of the play's imagery echoes the 'bardolatry' that has dogged Shakespeare criticism ever since the Romantics of the early nineteenth century. Notwithstanding such flaws, her work is immensely valuable in encouraging the study of imagery which is such a distinctive feature of every Shakespeare play. You can find more on imagery in the Language section, pages 76–9.

An example of criticism which uses a particular concept or theme to approach the play is D J Palmer's *As You Like It and the Idea of Play*. Palmer detects 'the heart of the comedy' as 'a demonstration of man's natural propensity for play'. Although feminists can properly object to Palmer's use of 'man's', his focus on 'play' identifies an important aspect of *As You Like It*. Duke Senior and his court 'fleet the time carelessly' in the Forest of Arden; wrestling turns conflict into sport at Duke Frederick's court; and as Celia persuades Rosalind to abandon her melancholy and 'be merry' the two women 'devise sports'. As Palmer notes:

> Before we reach Arden, therefore, we are given some anticipation of the nature of play, and of the equivocal relations between fiction and reality, game and earnest, folly and wisdom.

Palmer argues that Shakespeare 'is also playing games with his own art' in the play. He uses parody and burlesque, and creates the forest as 'this wide and universal theatre' in which Touchstone comments with playful scepticism on all he sees, and the various mating games are played out. Most notable is the mock courtship of Rosalind and Orlando, a play-world created by Rosalind's witty counterfeiting as Ganymede. And even though the cynical Jaques might be seen as the one character who lacks the capacity for play, Palmer judges him as a detached observer, to whom

> life has indeed become no more than a play, as he declares in his speech on the seven ages of man. 'All the world's a stage', and he is its spectator.

C L Barber sees Shakespeare developing a style of 'festive comedy'. Here, characters achieve understanding through the release afforded by 'saturnalia': living for a time in a world where conventional values and behaviour are overturned. The Forest of Arden offers that liberty. Other topsy-turvy worlds in Shakespeare's plays include the wood near Athens (*A Midsummer Night's Dream*), Illyria (*Twelfth Night*), and Falstaff's comedy and misrule (*King Henry IV Parts 1 and 2*).

Barber argues that in such 'holiday' places and atmospheres, characters move 'through release to clarification'. The phrase identifies a process: freedom afforded by liberty from ordinary limitations ('release') eventually results in clear-sighted understanding and relationships ('clarification'). Temporary disorder produces order. For Barber, the Forest of Arden is 'a festive place where the folly of romance can have its day'. He sees Shakespeare, through Touchstone and Jaques, making fun of Arden's pastoral innocence and romantic love rather than satirising his own contemporary world. Barber's remarks on Rosalind illustrate how traditional character criticism is integrated with the identification of themes:

> Romantic participation in love and humorous detachment from its follies, the two polar attitudes which are balanced against each other in the action as a whole, meet and are reconciled in Rosalind's personality. Because she remains aware of love's illusions while she herself is swept along by its deepest currents, she possesses as an attribute of character the power of combining wholehearted feeling and undistorted judgement, which gives the play its value.

Harold Bloom is the most recent critic to write in the tradition of Bradley's character criticism. In *Shakespeare: The Invention of the Human*, Bloom argues that Shakespeare's characters provided the self-reflexive models by which human beings first acquired selves to reflect on (or to put it more simply, Shakespeare's characters first showed us how to think about ourselves). That enormous claim about the origin of our subjectivity is disputed by almost all scholars, many of whom are dismissive of Bloom's character study approach as gushing and exaggerated.

Bloom's overriding concern with character is evident. He regards Orlando as 'an amiable young Hercules', and Touchstone is 'rancidly vicious' whereas Jaques is 'merely rancid'. Rosalind sends Bloom into hymns of praise. She is 'harmoniously balanced and beautifully sane', 'vital and beautiful, in spirit, in body, in mind', 'the most admirable person in all Shakespeare', an 'educational genius'. It is almost as if the critic has fallen in love with a fictional character, seeing her as a real person. Bloom also displays two other characteristics of an older critical style as he finds moral lessons in the play and confidently uses the first person plural ('us') as if everyone shared his own feelings for Rosalind:

> she instructs us in the miracle of being a harmonious consciousness that is also able to accommodate the reality of another self

But if many modern critics condemn Bloom for his style and judgements, he is, in return, contemptuously dismissive of current critical developments. His comment on what he calls sexual politics ('one of the most hideous of our current critical fashions') can serve to introduce the next section. It aptly demonstrates the strong feelings that more modern criticism can evoke:

> Rosalind has been appropriated by our current specialists in gender politics, who sometimes even give us a lesbian Rosalind, more occupied with Celia (or even Phebe) than with poor Orlando.

Modern criticism

Throughout the second half of the twentieth century and in the twenty-first, critical approaches to Shakespeare have radically challenged the style and assumptions of the traditional approaches described above. New critical approaches argue that traditional interpretations, with their focus on character, are individualistic and misleading. The traditional concentration on personal feelings ignores society and history, and so divorces literary, dramatic and aesthetic matters from their social context. Further, their detachment from the real world makes them elitist, sexist and unpolitical.

Modern critical perspectives therefore shift the focus from individuals to how social conditions (of the world of the play and of Shakespeare's England) are reflected in characters' relationships, language and behaviour. Modern criticism also concerns itself with how changing social assumptions at different periods of time have affected interpretations of the play. That change is remarked on by Penny Gay, who described in 1999 how she might once have written in the style of traditional criticism:

> Thirty years ago I might have written an elegant essay on *As You Like It* and the human desire for wholeness through marriage and incorporation into a regenerated community

Penny Gay's current reading of *As You Like It* is discussed below (page 99). Here it is significant, however, to note that *As You Like It*, like other comedies, apart from *The Merchant of Venice*, has attracted less radical critical attention than the tragedies. Further, certain aspects of modern criticism have featured strongly in traditional criticism of *As You Like It*, notably in identifying the Elizabethan contexts and relevances of the play, and in noting that the Forest of Arden is not an entirely benign place. This section will explore how recent critical approaches to Shakespeare can or have been used to address *As You Like It*. Like traditional criticism, contemporary perspectives include many different approaches but share common features. Modern criticism:

- is sceptical of 'character' approaches;
- concentrates on political, social and economic factors (arguing that these factors determine Shakespeare's creativity and audiences' and critics' interpretations);
- identifies contradictions, fragmentation and disunity in the plays;
- questions the possibility of 'happy' or 'hopeful' endings, preferring ambiguous, unsettling or sombre endings;
- produces readings that are subversive of existing social structures;
- identifies how the plays express the interests of dominant groups, particularly rich and powerful males;
- insists that 'theory' (psychological, social, etc.) is essential to produce valid readings;
- often expresses its commitment (for example, to feminism, or equality, or political change);
- argues all readings are political or ideological readings (and that traditional criticism falsely claims to be objective);
- argues that traditional approaches have always interpreted Shakespeare conservatively, in ways that confirm and maintain the interests of the elite or dominant class.

The following discussion is organised under headings which represent major contemporary critical perspectives (political, feminist, performance, psychoanalytic, postmodern). But it is vital to appreciate that there is often overlap between the categories, and that to pigeonhole any example of criticism too precisely is to reduce its value and application.

Political criticism

'Political criticism' is a convenient label for approaches concerned with power and social structure: in the world of the play, in

Shakespeare's time and in our own. At first sight *As You Like It* appears to be resistant to such interpretations, being centrally concerned with love. Nonetheless, various interpretations both in criticism and in stage productions have highlighted 'political' aspects of the play. The most obvious focus concentrates on the violent and oppressive society from which Rosalind and Celia, Orlando and Adam flee. In contrast, Marilyn French, in *Shakespeare's Division of Experience*, argues that the play is concerned with 'the underside of society, made up of women, exiles, outcasts, the poor, the eccentric, and the low in status'.

Other 'political' approaches have been noted on page 68, in Stephen Unwin's view that the play reflects contemporary anxieties about political power and profiteering, and on page 69, in Richard Wilson's argument that *As You Like It* is Shakespeare's dramatisation of agrarian conflict, reflecting contemporary rioting against enclosures. Focusing on a particular line, Penny Gay suggests that Elizabethan audiences at the Globe may well have experienced 'a frisson of political radicalism' in the reference to Robin Hood, the outlaw who robbed the rich to help the poor. But it is important to notice that the exiles in the forest do no such thing. They do not rob the rich to help the poor, or right injustice. They only play. Placing that fact in a much wider perspective, Alan Sinfield is insistently 'political' in his interpretation of the play:

> The forest people in *As You Like It* do not, actually, 'fleet the time carelessly'. They have hierarchy, property and money, and give little serious thought to living without them. Despite his sturdy independence, Orlando would rather subject himself to his brother's malice than take to the roads without money . . . luckily he has Adam's saving and service, so he can travel in the style of a gentleman . . . The outlaw band maintain, with scarcely a second thought, the hierarchy they observed at court . . . (They) are not outside the state system; they are a government in waiting. The play presents a conflict within the ruling elite: which faction is to control the state and its resources?

Such interpretations use Amiens' song telling of 'man's ingratitude' to draw attention to the conflicts of the court, where brother is set against brother, and ambition, envy and intrigue are common. Duke Frederick has usurped his brother, and he exiles Rosalind on pain of death. He leads an army to destroy his brother's life, and only the fairy-tale intervention of 'an old religious man' prevents brutal political murder. The 'icy fang' of the winds of the Forest of Arden is seen as a metaphor for social relationships. The man who employs Corin is a hard taskmaster, and Duke Senior's exiled court is far from being an egalitarian community. At the play's end the old political power structure is restored as the exiles are only too happy to return to court.

A well-known critic who is often called on in support of political interpretations of Shakespeare's plays is the Polish scholar Jan Kott. Kott fought with the Polish army and underground movement against the Nazis in the Second World War (1939–45), and had direct experience of the suffering and terror caused by Stalinist repression in Poland in the years after the war. His book, *Shakespeare our Contemporary*, saw parallels between the violence and cruelty of the modern world and the worlds of tyranny and despair that Shakespeare depicted in his tragedies.

Kott's discussion of *As You Like It* is much concerned with the confusions of desire that arise from cross-dressing. For him, 'the love scenes in the Forest of Arden have the logic of dreams' and 'eroticism goes through bodies like an electric current'. But Kott's discussion of the Forest of Arden, significantly contained in a chapter titled 'Shakespeare's bitter Arcadia', goes beyond noting its dream-like qualities ('speeded up', 'violent', 'metaphorically meaningful') to identify its political significance. It is a place of

> escape from the cruel kingdom where, as always in
> Shakespeare, two themes obsessively repeat themselves: the
> exile of a lawful prince and the depriving a younger brother of
> his inheritance. For Shakespeare this is rudimentary social
> history in a nutshell.

Kott comments on the 'singularly dark' opening of the play, in which 'a tyrant has ascended the throne, a brother persecutes his brother, love and friendship have been destroyed by ambition, the world is ruled by sheer force and money'. He finds parallels with the Histories: 'everyone is afraid. The new prince is distrustful, suspicious, jealous of everything and everybody, unsure of his position, sensing the enemy in everyone'. Escape to the Forest of Arden is, for Kott, to find similar qualities: 'The kingdom of nature is equally ruthless and egoistic as the world of civilisation. There is no return to primeval harmony'.

Kott considers the Forest of Arden to be 'a real forest, as well as a feudal utopia and a sneering comment on that utopia'. He passes harsh judgement on the episode in which Rosalind and Celia encounter Corin, and buy the cottage, land and sheep:

> The Forest of Arden, where the golden age was to come anew, is ruled by the capitalist laws of hire . . . Arcadia has been turned into real estate, into landed property.

Although Kott acknowledges the fictional nature of Arden and the lyricism of Rosalind's love, his vision is one of gloomy pessimism. But even though his arguments have been much contested for their contradictoriness, and his style criticised for its over-dramatic emphasis, his judgements possess a gritty realism to balance against traditional and romantic views of the play.

Feminist criticism

Feminism aims to achieve rights and equality for women in social, political and economic life. It challenges sexism: those beliefs and practices which result in the degradation, oppression and subordination of women. Feminist critics therefore reject 'male ownership' of criticism in which men determined what questions were to be asked of a play, and which answers were acceptable. They argue that male criticism often neglects, represses or misrepresents female experience, and stereotypes or distorts women's points of view.

Shakespeare's comedies hold special interest for feminist critics. Unlike the tragedies or Histories, women characters have the major parts, and speak as many words as men. They are witty and intelligent, more than holding their own with men in dialogue, and their actions powerfully influence or direct the development of plot. Some, like Rosalind, appear to be independent spirits, free to act in their dramatic worlds, apparently unshackled by father, husband or lover.

In the comedies, several female characters adopt male disguise to achieve their purposes: Viola in *Twelfth Night*, Julia in *The Two*

Gentlemen of Verona, Portia in *The Merchant of Venice*, and Rosalind. For feminist critics, such cross-dressing and gender ambiguity raise important questions of sexual politics and gender construction. Those issues are complicated by the fact that in Elizabethan times female roles were played by males. Some feminists argue that because of this, Rosalind's cross-dressing had enhanced erotic effect on Elizabethan audiences. At the play's end, the sight of males (playing Rosalind, Celia, Phebe and Audrey) marrying males (Orlando, Oliver, Silvius and Touchstone) opened up alternatives to the conventional view that marriage is a natural and desired outcome of comedy (and of real life). Such issues have increasingly influenced stage performances, as shown on page 103 under 'Performance criticism'.

Feminist criticism, like any 'approach', takes a wide variety of forms. Nonetheless, it is possible to identify major concerns for feminist writing on *As You Like It*. It insists on the importance of 'female agency' in the play: Rosalind's actions are largely responsible for the play's outcomes. Further, the friendship of Rosalind and Celia is seen as a key example of female bonding, as strong as the male friendships celebrated in Elizabethan life and drama. But some feminists argue that Rosalind abandons Celia for Orlando, thus weakening the female bonding the play demonstrates so notably in its first half.

Feminists also note that the play is remarkable for its 'absent mothers'. There is no mention of Rosalind's, Celia's or Orlando's mother. In contrast, all three have fathers who strongly affect the action of the play (even though Orlando's father is dead). The absence of mothers is a common feature of many of Shakespeare's plays, and reveals much about the lower status of women in Elizabethan England.

Most commonly, feminists approach the play using the notion of patriarchy: male domination of women. Feminists point to the fact that throughout history, power has been in the hands of men, both in society and in the family. Feminist criticism therefore makes much of the fact that although *As You Like It* has as its main character a female who seems to break free of such control, and shows she is more than an equal to all the men she encounters, nonetheless, at the play's end, Rosalind willingly seeks marriage. That acceptance of marriage would, in Shakespeare's time, mean subjugation to her husband's authority.

A major question for feminist criticism is whether Shakespeare's female characters confirm or subvert Elizabethan negative stereotypes of women as weak, submissive and pliable. Feminists argue that *As You Like It* challenges such stereotyping, and shows, in Rosalind, that it can be transcended, as Rosalind and Celia escape patriarchal control and flourish in Arden. Penny Gay's discussion of *As You Like It* makes many points that illustrate a feminist approach to the play. They include the following:

- The pursuit of power, status and affluence is the dominant drive of the males who rule the world of Act 1.
- Masculine language pervades even the women's speeches: Rosalind's plan to dress 'at all points like a man' includes 'doubly phallic weaponry'.
- Hunting in the forest portrays 'the ideology of machismo'. Killing deer symbolises the violent and competitive ideology of masculinity.
- Rosalind and Celia create 'a gendered feminine offstage space' in Arden, 'like fringe upon a petticoat'.
- When Celia buys the cottage, pasture and flock, the play presented to Elizabethan audiences the radical notion of women owning and working property.
- The all-male outlawed court lives deep within the forest. Rosalind and Celia live 'in the skirts of the forest' in a 'bottom' (good pasture land) which is 'a recognisably feminine topographical feature as opposed to the phallic stands of trees of the deep woods'.
- The courtship scenes are charged with both heterosexual and homoerotic feeling. The multiple erotic possibilities appeal to audiences as much as Rosalind's wit and charm.
- The bloody napkin that causes Rosalind to faint is not only a symbol of the absent, wounded Orlando. It is 'a metonym of her own hidden femininity'. (A metonym replaces the name of a person or thing by the name of an attribute or something closely connected with the person or thing.)
- Violence as a characteristic of dominant masculinity invades even the language of traditional pastoral love in the dialogue of Phebe and Silvius in Act 3 Scene 6, lines 1–31 ('executioner', 'death', 'bloody drops', 'injure', 'murder' and so on).

Gay's interpretation perceives both Arden and Elizabethan theatre as marginal and excitingly libertarian places, especially for women. But, like all feminist critics, she notes the limits of such 'liberty', particularly in Rosalind's willing submission to her father and husband in her repeated 'To you I give myself, for I am yours' (Act 5 Scene 4, lines 101–2). But, again like many feminist critics, Gay argues that the play can be seen as presenting an ambivalent attitude to marriage because of the three 'wedding ceremonies' it portrays, raising questions of the relationship between the wedding ritual and the realities of the social world. First, Touchstone and Audrey encounter the incompetent Sir Oliver Martext, who proves incapable of marrying them. Second, the climax of the wooing scene (Act 4 Scene 1) casts Celia as a female priest, a notion that defies and offends patriarchal authority (only males could become priests). The third wedding scene in the final act can present Hymen in ways which 'can either reinforce or subvert the incorporation of Rosalind back into the patriarchal order represented by the father/uncle Duke Senior'.

Gay's readings, like all critical interpretations, raise the question of whether they are what Shakespeare intended. Was he purposefully challenging female stereotyping? Whilst many critics today argue that Shakespeare's intentions can never be known, a distinctive feature of feminist criticism is to suggest that *As You Like It* and the other comedies subject patriarchal conventions to critical scrutiny, exposing them as irrational and repressive. The implication is that *As You Like It* shows that love can be a partnership of equals, and that women's desires and capacity for feeling are the same as men's, not inferior to them.

Performance criticism

Performance criticism fully acknowledges that *As You Like It* is a play: a script to be performed by actors to an audience. It examines all aspects of the play in performance: its staging in the theatre or on film and video. Performance criticism focuses on Shakespeare's stagecraft and the semiotics of theatre (words, costumes, gestures, etc.), together with the 'afterlife' of the play (what happened to *As You Like It* after Shakespeare wrote it). That involves scrutiny of how productions at different periods have presented the play. As such, performance criticism appraises how the text has been cut, added to, rewritten and rearranged to present a version felt appropriate to the times.

There is no written evidence of a performance of *As You Like It* in Shakespeare's lifetime, or indeed for over 130 years after his death. There is a tradition that it was the very first play acted at the Globe Theatre on London's Bankside and that Shakespeare played Adam in that production. Another tradition claims that *As You Like It* was performed before King James I in 1603. But no one knows for sure if these stories are true.

The first historical record of a performance is of an adaptation in 1723, *Love in a Forest*. This cut out all the lower-class characters, substituted fencing with rapiers for the wrestling match, and included lines, songs and characters from other Shakespeare plays. Jaques married Celia, and the mechanicals from *A Midsummer Night's Dream* performed their Pyramus and Thisbe play.

The first recorded performance of the play largely as Shakespeare had written it was in 1740 at London's Theatre Royal, Drury Lane. From that time the play has been enduringly popular onstage. Unlike in Shakespeare's own theatre, females now played women's roles, and the cross-dressing or 'breeches parts' proved very appealing to audiences and actresses alike. The leading actresses of each generation played Rosalind, (one, Peg Woffington, even suffered a near-fatal stroke whilst speaking the Epilogue). Throughout the eighteenth and nineteenth centuries the performance history of the play to a large extent comprises reactions to portrayals of the major character, often displaying fascinated interest in Ganymede's costume and legs.

In the nineteenth century, portrayals of Rosalind became increasingly romantic. In contrast to the tomboy or hoyden conception popular in the eighteenth century, the Victorians valued a tender but passionate performance of the role, combining merriment with innate dignity, high spirits with grace. The text would be cut or amended to facilitate such portrayals. For example, Rosalind's remark that her sadness comes from thoughts of her 'child's father' (Act 1 Scene 3, line 8) was considered indecent, and was altered to 'my father's child' (Rosalind herself).

Nineteenth-century productions of *As You Like It* relished the opportunity for elaborate sets, costumes, spectacle and music to stress the festive and pastoral aspects of the play. An 1842 production had a cast of 97, and a background of a huge turreted castle. Duke Frederick made a grand processional entry to see the wrestling match. Such features, intended as a kind of historical realism (which in practice meant only a stereotyped view of an earlier 'Merry England'), involved frequent and time-consuming scene changes. The result was that Shakespeare's text was often heavily cut.

Attempts were made to portray a 'realistic' Forest of Arden. By the end of the nineteenth century a profusion of trees, logs, ferns and plants filled the stage, which was often covered in leaves. A rippling brook was a common sight, and sheep, rabbits and even deer made an appearance. For many years at Stratford-upon-Avon, productions of *As You Like It* included a stuffed deer from nearby Charlecote Park, where Shakespeare was supposed to have poached deer, and fled to London to escape the wrath of the landowner. In 1919 the director of that year's production refused to include the stuffed deer. Many local people were outraged at the break with tradition, and the director was insulted in the street.

The twentieth century saw a return to much simpler stagings of the play. Although the tradition of extravagant productions lingered on, most no longer attempted to create an impression of realism. Under the influence of William Poel and Harley Granville-Barker the stage was cleared of the clutter of historical detail. The aim was to recapture the conditions of the Elizabethan bare stage, which was not dependent on theatrical illusion. That implied a minimum of scenery, scenes flowing swiftly into each other, and a concern for clear speaking of Shakespeare's language.

In the second half of the twentieth century, the earlier emphasis on the play as mainly a starring vehicle for the actress playing Rosalind gave way to 'company productions' in which all the actors contributed significantly to the success of each performance.

Social issues have also been prominently stressed in some modern productions, in the emphasis on the harsh political realities of Duke Frederick's court and the exploitation of the natural world by the exiled court. The 1978 BBC TV production was shot in the grounds of Glamis castle in Scotland, but a 1996 film set Arden in a modern urban wasteland.

As You Like It is also popular outside England. In Italy, Salvador Dalí designed surrealist sets for a production in Rome. Before the reunification of Germany, a famous 1977 production in Berlin implied that the Forest of Arden (a 'free' place) was like West Berlin surrounded by the socialist German Democratic Republic. The production included appearances of Robin Hood and Robinson Crusoe.

It is impossible to detail the great variety of ways in which *As You Like It* has been performed throughout the twentieth and into the twenty-first century. Some productions have portrayed a lesbian relationship between Rosalind and Celia (the feature that so vexes Harold Bloom, see page 93). Such a portrayal is just one indication of an aspect of the play that became increasingly the focus of attention: gender. As noted on page 98, *As You Like It* raises crucial questions of gender: the assumptions a society possesses about what it is to be male or female. Such assumptions are socially constructed, not natural. Thus, when Rosalind cross-dresses as a male, the audience becomes aware that her disguise challenges conventional beliefs about how a man or woman is expected to behave. That challenge acquires extra complexity when the actor playing Rosalind is male, as in Shakespeare's time.

Two much-praised twentieth-century all-male productions made those complexities apparent to modern audiences. The 1967 National Theatre production, in dress, behaviour and style, expressed the 'swinging sixties' attitudes of the time in blurring distinctions between male and female. In 1995 the Cheek by Jowl all-male production was acclaimed by some critics as demonstrating that love transcends sexual (physical) and gender (socially constructed) differences. In both productions the male actor playing Rosalind was praised for avoiding a camp or homosexual interpretation of the role.

But it is only fair to note that both productions also attracted negative criticism. Some critics (both feminist and others) judged aspects of both as gender caricatures: 'arch', 'bimbo-like' and 'false'. Such different judgements of the same productions is testament both to Shakespeare's enduring capacity for varied interpretation and to the fact that the values and attitudes a critic or spectator already possesses will strongly influence what he or she 'sees'. For example, the praise for the 1995 production included such contrasting phrases as 'nothing glibly homoerotic' and an 'unabashed celebration of gay desire'. Just as criticism reflects the political beliefs of the critic, so too on the fraught question of gender, people often see what they wish to see.

Psychoanalytic criticism

In the twentieth century, psychoanalysis became a major influence on the understanding and interpretation of human behaviour. The founder of psychoanalysis, Sigmund Freud, explained personality as the result of unconscious and irrational desires, repressed memories or wishes, sexuality, fantasy, anxiety and conflict. Freud's theories have had a strong influence on criticism and stagings of Shakespeare's plays, most obviously on *Hamlet*, in the well-known claim that Hamlet suffers from an Oedipus complex.

As You Like It has attracted comparatively little psychoanalytic critical writing. As Norman Holland points out, such critics usually discuss the play through analysis of characters. Holland's book, *Psychoanalysis and Shakespeare*, details only brief accounts of psychoanalytic interpretations of Jaques. They variously claim that he 'has an overdeveloped superego that makes him project his own failings on others'; that he suffers from depression; or that he is a 'thinking introvert', contrasted with the 'feeling extroverts' of Touchstone and Orlando. Occasionally a psychoanalytic approach can be detected in a stage production. For example, the 1985 Royal Shakespeare production staged the hunting scene (Act 4 Scene 2) as Celia's dream of male violence and defloration, which one critic saw as 'feared yet desired'.

Such interpretations reveal the obvious weaknesses in applying psychoanalytic theories to *As You Like It*. They cannot be proved or disproved, they neglect historical, political and social factors which are fundamental to the play, and they are highly speculative. Psychoanalytic approaches are therefore often accused of imposing interpretations based on theory rather than upon Shakespeare's text. But the play's evident interest in cross-dressing may prove amenable to developing possible psychoanalytic interpretations.

Postmodern criticism

Postmodern criticism (sometimes called 'deconstruction' or 'post-structuralism') is not always easy to understand because it is not centrally concerned with consistency or reasoned argument. It does not accept that one section of the story is necessarily connected to what follows, or that characters relate to each other in meaningful ways. Because of such assumptions, postmodern criticism is sometimes described as 'reading against the grain' or less politely as 'textual harassment'. The approach therefore has obvious drawbacks in providing a model for examination students, who are expected to display reasoned, coherent argument, and respect for the evidence of the text.

Postmodern approaches to *As You Like It* are most clearly seen in stage productions. There, you could think of it as simply 'a mixture of styles'. The label 'postmodern' is applied to productions which self-consciously show little regard for consistency in character, or for coherence in telling the story. Characters are dressed in costumes from very different historical periods. Ironically, Shakespeare himself has been regarded as a postmodern writer in the way he mixes genres in his plays, comedy with tragedy.

Productions which update settings to modern times have also been considered postmodern. Here, the clearest example is Christine Edzard's 1996 production of *As You Like It*, which sets the play in the 1990s, making Frederick's court a corporate business emporium and the forest an urban wasteland. Some critics found the film perverse, because they felt that the contemporary setting was at odds with Shakespeare's language and the tradition of pastoral romance. But Amelia Marriette values how Edzard calls traditional assumptions into question, and argues that the film 'can only be fully appreciated when assessed in its own avant-garde terms as a postmodern experiment'.

Some critics focus on minor or marginal characters, or on gaps or silences in the play. They claim that these features, previously overlooked as unimportant, reveal significant truths about the play. But postmodern criticism most typically revels in the cleverness of its own use of language, and accepts all kinds of anomalies and contradictions in a spirit of playfulness or 'carnival'. It abandons any notion of the organic unity of the play, and rejects the assumption that a Shakespeare play possesses clear patterns or themes. Some postmodern critics even deny the possibility of finding meaning in language. They claim that words simply refer to other words, and so any interpretation is endlessly delayed (or 'deferred' as the deconstructionists say).

Such postmodern critics make much of what they call 'the instability of language'. In practice this often means little more than traditional notions of ambiguity: that words can have different meanings. It has long been accepted that Shakespeare's language has multiple, not single meanings. In *As You Like It*, that openness to multiple meanings is perhaps most clearly seen in Hymen's line 'If truth holds true contents' (Act 5 Scene 4, line 114). Malcolm Evans, in his demanding post-structuralist reading of *As You Like It*, claims the line has at least 168 possible meanings. In a style typical of such readings, Evans declares the line makes

> gestures towards the truth contained at the heart of truth, identical with itself, only to break down in a delirium of wordplays on 'truth', 'holds', 'true', and 'contents' which leave no centre but tautology, endless supplementation, and a textual process whose closure can only be as you like it. The truth about such texts is inevitably conditional, inscribed in contradiction and absence, the work of the poet who affirms 'nothing'.

Organising your responses

The purpose of this section is to help you improve your writing about *As You Like It*. It offers practical guidance on two kinds of tasks: writing about an extract from the play and writing an essay. Whether you are answering an examination question, preparing coursework (term papers), or carrying out research into your own chosen topic, this section will help you organise and present your responses.

In all your writing, there are three vital things to remember:

- *As You Like It* is a play. Although it is usually referred to as a 'text', *As You Like It* is not a book, but a script intended to be acted on a stage. So your writing should demonstrate an awareness of the play in performance as theatre. That means you should always try to read the play with an 'inner eye', thinking about how it could look and sound onstage. The next best thing to seeing an actual production is to imagine yourself sitting in the audience, watching and listening to *As You Like It* being performed. By doing so, you will be able to write effectively about Shakespeare's language and dramatic techniques.

- *As You Like It* is not a presentation of 'reality'. It is a dramatic construct in which the playwright, through theatre, engages the emotions and intellect of the audience. The characters and story may persuade an audience to suspend its disbelief for several hours. The audience may identify with the characters, be deeply moved by them, and may think of them as if they are living human beings. However, when you write, a major part of your task is to show how Shakespeare achieves his dramatic effects that so engage the audience. Through discussion of his handling of language, character and plot, your writing reveals how Shakespeare uses themes and ideas, attitudes and values, to give insight into crucial social, moral and political dilemmas of his time – and yours.

- How Shakespeare learned his craft. As a schoolboy, and in his early years as a dramatist, Shakespeare used all kinds of models or frameworks to guide his writing. But he quickly learned how to vary and adapt the models to his own dramatic purposes. This section offers frameworks that you can use to structure your writing. As you use them, follow Shakespeare's example! Adapt them to suit your own writing style and needs.

Writing about an extract

It is an expected part of all Shakespeare study that you should be able to write well about an extract (sometimes called a 'passage') from the play. An extract is usually between 30 and 70 lines long, and you are invited to comment on it. The instructions vary. Sometimes the task is very briefly expressed:

- Write a detailed commentary on the following passage.
  or
- Write about the effect of the extract on your own thoughts and feelings.

At other times a particular focus is specified for your writing:

- With close reference to the language and imagery of the passage, show in what ways it helps to establish important issues in the play.
  or
- Analyse the style and structure of the extract, showing what it contributes to your appreciation of the play's major concerns.

In writing your response, you must of course take account of the precise wording of the task, and ensure you concentrate on each particular point specified. But however the invitation to write about an extract is expressed, it requires you to comment in detail on the language. You should identify and evaluate how the language reveals character, contributes to plot development, offers opportunities for dramatic effect, and embodies crucial concerns of the play as a whole. These 'crucial concerns' are also referred to as the 'themes' or 'issues' or 'preoccupations' of the play.

The following framework is a guide to how you can write a detailed commentary on an extract. Writing a paragraph on each item will help you bring out the meaning and significance of the extract, and show how Shakespeare achieves his effects.

> **Paragraph 1:** Locate the extract in the play and say who is onstage.
> **Paragraph 2:** State what the extract is about and identify its structure.
> **Paragraph 3:** Identify the mood or atmosphere of the extract.
> **Paragraphs 4–8:** ⎫ These paragraphs analyse how
>   Diction (vocabulary) ⎪ Shakespeare achieves his effects. They
>   Imagery ⎬ concentrate on the language of the
>   Antithesis ⎪ extract, showing the dramatic effect of
>   Repetition ⎪ each item, and how the language
>   Lists ⎭ expresses crucial concerns of the play.
> **Paragraph 9:** Staging opportunities
> **Paragraph 10:** Conclusion

The following example uses the framework to show how the paragraphs making up the essay might be written. The framework headings (in bold) would not, of course, appear in your essay. They are presented only to help you see how the framework is used.

Extract

ROSALIND   Am not I your Rosalind?

ORLANDO   I take some joy to say you are, because I would be talking of her.

ROSALIND   Well, in her person, I say I will not have you.

ORLANDO   Then, in mine own person, I die.   5

ROSALIND   No, faith, die by attorney. The poor world is almost six thousand years old and in all this time there was not any man died in his own person, videlicet, in a love-cause. Troilus had his brains dashed out with a Grecian club, yet he did what he could to die before, and he is one of the patterns of love;   10 Leander, he would have lived many a fair year though Hero had turned nun, if it had not been for a hot midsummer night, for, good youth, he went but forth to wash him in the Hellespont and, being taken with the cramp, was drowned, and the foolish chroniclers of that age found it was Hero of Sestos. But these   15 are all lies: men have died from time to time – and worms have eaten them – but not for love.

ORLANDO   I would not have my right Rosalind of this mind, for I protest her frown might kill me.

ROSALIND   By this hand, it will not kill a fly. But come, now I will   20
        be your Rosalind in a more coming-on disposition and, ask me
        what you will, I will grant it.
ORLANDO   Then love me, Rosalind.
ROSALIND   Yes, faith, will I, Fridays and Saturdays and all.
ORLANDO   And wilt thou have me?   25
ROSALIND   Aye, and twenty such.
ORLANDO   What sayest thou?
ROSALIND   Are you not good?
ORLANDO   I hope so.
ROSALIND   Why then, can one desire too much of a good thing? –   30
        Come, sister, you shall be the priest and marry us. – Give me
        your hand, Orlando. – What do you say, sister?
ORLANDO   Pray thee marry us.
CELIA   I cannot say the words.
ROSALIND   You must begin: 'Will you, Orlando – '   35
CELIA   Go to. – Will you, Orlando, have to wife this Rosalind?
ORLANDO   I will.
ROSALIND   Aye, but when?
ORLANDO   Why, now, as fast as she can marry us.
ROSALIND   Then you must say, 'I take thee, Rosalind, for wife.'   40
ORLANDO   I take thee, Rosalind, for wife.
ROSALIND   I might ask you for your commission, but I do take thee,
        Orlando, for my husband. There's a girl goes before the priest,
        and certainly a woman's thought runs before her actions.
ORLANDO   So do all thoughts: they are winged.   45
ROSALIND   Now, tell me how long you would have her after you
        have possessed her?
ORLANDO   For ever and a day.
ROSALIND   Say a day without the 'ever'. No, no, Orlando: men are
        April when they woo, December when they wed; maids are May   50
        when they are maids, but the sky changes when they are wives.
        I will be more jealous of thee than a Barbary cock-pigeon over
        his hen; more clamorous than a parrot against rain, more new-
        fangled than an ape; more giddy in my desires than a monkey. I
        will weep for nothing, like Diana in the fountain, and I will do   55
        that when you are disposed to be merry. I will laugh like a
        hyena, and that when thou art inclined to sleep.
ORLANDO   But will my Rosalind do so?

ROSALIND   By my life, she will do as I do.

ORLANDO   O, but she is wise.   60

ROSALIND   Or else she could not have the wit to do this: the wiser,
the waywarder. Make the doors upon a woman's wit, and it will
out at the casement; shut that, and 'twill out at the key hole;
stop that, 'twill fly with the smoke out at the chimney.

(Act 4 Scene 1, lines 70–132)

Paragraph 1: Locate the extract in the play and say who is onstage.

In the Forest of Arden Rosalind, disguised as the youth Ganymede,
has persuaded Orlando to woo her and so cure him of love. The mock
wooing has begun. Orlando thinks he is playing a game, pretending
that Ganymede is Rosalind. But it really is Rosalind he woos, and she,
deeply in love with Orlando, relishes the opportunity to enjoy his
loving. But her cousin Celia, disguised as the shepherdess Aliena, is
not amused at the pretence.

Paragraph 2: State what the extract is about and identify its structure.

(Begin with one or two sentences identifying what the extract is about,
followed by several sentences briefly identifying its structure, that is,
the unfolding events and the different sections of the extract.)

The extract shows Rosalind teasing Orlando, questioning whether
he really is in love, then playing out a marriage ceremony that he
thinks is a game but which reveals her true desire to be his wife. The
extract has several sections. First Rosalind deflates Orlando's ideal of
love. Next she contrives the pretend marriage. Then she says how
marriage cools men's affections, and tells how capriciously she will
behave when she is married. She claims it is impossible to control a
woman's wit.

Paragraph 3: Identify the mood or atmosphere of the extract.

High spirits and dramatic irony pervade the extract. Rosalind bubbles
with imaginative invention, delighting in every moment of her
pretence. But she, Celia and the audience know what Orlando does
not, that he really is wooing and marrying Rosalind. That dramatic
irony adds to the comedy, as Rosalind both teases and speaks truly.

Paragraph 4: Diction

Much of the language is plain and easily understood, because

Rosalind uses her disguise to allow her to speak what she sincerely feels. But at times she uses less common words to increase the authority of what she says. To give weight to her plain conclusion that 'men have died from time to time . . . but not for love', she uses 'attorney' (proxy), 'videlicet' (namely) and the names of legendary characters. She similarly uses 'commission' (authority). Her speech on her future giddy behaviour as a wife uses examples that were familiar Elizabethan beliefs (that male pigeons were jealous, parrots noisy before rain, and so on). Her use of 'wit' created sexual interpretations for Elizabethans because it was slang for female genitalia.

Paragraph 5: Imagery

Rosalind uses images from classical mythology to prove that men die from any cause but love. Troilus and Leander were famous lovers, but both died violently. Like so much of the play, the images debunk the pastoral romance assumption of dying for love, as does Rosalind's denial that her frown would kill a fly, let alone Orlando (just as Phebe had earlier mocked the belief). Rosalind's seasonal imagery of how men cool after marriage is sardonically vivid: April in wooing, December after marriage. She uses more nature imagery to describe women ('May', 'sky changes') and how capriciously she will behave as a wife: as easily distracted as an ape, irritatingly noisy as a hyena and so on. Her image of Diana in the fountain recalls a famous London statue. All such images also puncture the concept of romantic love.

Paragraph 6: Antithesis

The previous paragraph noted striking oppositions as Shakespeare sets word against word to increase dramatic tension and humour: 'April' versus 'December', 'May' versus 'sky changes', dying for love versus death itself. Such antitheses contrast the ideals of romantic love against practical realities. The whole extract, like the play itself, visually celebrates antithesis as appearance conflicts with reality in Rosalind's disguise as Ganymede. Her very first words, setting 'I' against 'Rosalind' express that antithesis. Orlando does not see what he thinks he sees, and that fills almost every personal pronoun ('I', 'me') and 'Rosalind' with antithetical tension, adding to audience delight as they enjoy the ambiguity. In the theatre, Rosalind's oppositions of 'girl' against 'priest', and a woman's 'thought' against her 'actions' often evokes audience laughter.

Paragraph 7: Repetition
An obvious repetition of words chimes through Rosalind's description of how giddily she will behave when she is married ('more . . . than' and 'I will'), emphasising the waywardness of her behaviour. The repetition of the words of the marriage ceremony ('Will you', 'I take thee') intensifies the ritual significance of what is happening. There are also distinctive repetitions in the rhythms of the prose. Sections of dialogue echo each other, stressing the close relationship of Rosalind and Orlando. Each of Rosalind's three long speeches is rhythmically structured. In the final one, alliteration ('wit', 'wiser', 'waywarder'), word repetition ('will' / 'twill'), and rhythmical repetition as phrase echoes phrase ('Make', 'shut', 'stop') add to their humour and argumentative power.

Paragraph 8: Lists
Shakespeare's technique of piling item on item, event on event, is evident in each of Rosalind's three long speeches. The accumulation deepens the persuasive force of what she says about romantic heroes, her own behaviour, and women's wit. The sheer richness of detail creates vivid pictures that add to meaning. Troilus' and Leander's deaths disprove romantic love. Rosalind's promised impulsive changeability is conveyed in images of pigeons, parrots, apes and other creatures. And a woman's wit will simply escape in spite of all efforts to constrain it!

Paragraph 9: Staging opportunities
Amid all the verbal fireworks of Rosalind's imagination, the dramatic centre of the extract is the mock marriage ceremony. For an Elizabethan audience it held great significance, because a verbal contract of marriage before a third party was binding. Further, the sight of a woman acting as priest transgressed all bounds. No woman in real life could hold religious office. Today, the episode has great emotional significance. Although it is contained within comedy, it is usually staged at some length, in which the ritual, silences, and non-verbal behaviour, as much as the language, bring out the sheer depth of affection between Rosalind and Orlando.

Stagings also attempt to highlight as much as possible the dramatic irony of what is said and done throughout the extract. That does not mean that Rosalind winks at the audience, but that in a host of subtle and sensitive ways she implies that the audience is complicit in the deception being practised on Orlando. This might be achieved in her evident playfulness, or in a catch of the voice as she says 'Rosalind'.

Celia speaks only a few words, but she is crucial to the scene. In performance she shows just what she thinks of everything that Rosalind says and does (she is usually disapproving). She may feel that the close bond between her and Rosalind is now weakened beyond repair. Her 'Go to' can be spoken with genuine irritation at the deceit her cousin is asking her to practise.

Paragraph 10: Conclusion
The extract displays Rosalind's dazzling wit and impishness. She virtually runs rings round Orlando, mocking his illusions of romantic love, and is always in control of what is said and done. But for all the comedy, she has serious intentions, and uses her disguise as Ganymede to achieve her purposes: to get Orlando to declare his love to her, and to marry him. The gender ambiguities in this scene of a girl playing a boy playing a girl are made even more complex in all-male productions (as always in Shakespeare's time, and occasionally today). In such productions, the sight of two men vowing marriage expands even more the range of possible audience reactions, and so adds more significance to the claim of the play's title: *As You Like It*.

Reminders - writing about an extract
- The framework is only a guide. It helps you to structure your writing. Use the framework for practice on other extracts. Adapt as you feel appropriate. Make it your own.
- Structure your response in paragraphs. Each paragraph makes a particular point and helps build up your argument.
- Focus tightly on the language, especially vocabulary, imagery, antithesis, lists, repetitions.
- Remember that *As You Like It* is a play, a drama intended for performance. The purpose of writing about an extract is to identify how Shakespeare creates dramatic effect. What techniques does he use?

- Try to imagine the action. Visualise the scene in your mind's eye. But remember there can be many valid ways of performing a scene. Offer alternatives. Justify your own preferences by reference to the language.
- Who is onstage? Imagine their interaction. How do 'silent characters' react to what's said?
- Look for the theatrical qualities of the extract. What guides for actors' movement and expressions are given in the language? Comment on any stage directions.
- How might the audience respond? In Elizabethan times? Today? How might you respond as a member of the audience?
- How might the lines be spoken? Tone, emphasis, pace, pauses? Identify shifting moods and registers. Is the verse pattern smooth or broken, flowing or full of hesitations and abrupt turns?
- What is the importance of the extract in the play as a whole? Justify its thematic significance.
- Are there 'key words'?
- How does the extract develop the plot, reveal character, deepen themes?
- Offer a variety of interpretative opportunities.

Writing an essay

As part of your study of *As You Like It* you will be asked to write essays, either under examination conditions or for coursework (term papers). Examinations mean that you are under pressure of time, usually having around one hour to prepare and write each essay. Coursework means that you have much longer to think about and produce your essay. But whatever the type of essay, each will require you to develop an argument about a particular aspect of *As You Like It*.

Before suggesting a strategy for your essay-writing, it is helpful to recall just what an essay is. 'Essay' comes from the French *essai*: an attempt or a trial. It was originally used by the sixteenth-century French writer Montaigne (whose work Shakespeare certainly read). Montaigne used *essais* to attempt to find out what he thought about particular subjects, such as friendship, or cannibals or education. In each essay he used many practical examples to test his response to the topic.

The essays you write on *As You Like It* similarly require that you set out your thoughts on a particular aspect of the play, using evidence from the text. The people who read your essays (examiners, teachers, lecturers) will have certain expectations for your writing. In each essay they will expect you to discuss and analyse a particular topic, using evidence from the play to develop an argument in an organised, coherent and persuasive way. Examiners look for, and reward, what they call 'an informed personal response'. This simply means that you show you have good knowledge of the play ('informed') and can use evidence from it to support and justify your own viewpoint ('personal').

You can write about *As You Like It* from different points of view. As pages 93–106 show, you can approach the play from a number of critical perspectives (feminist, political, psychoanalytic, etc.). You can also set the play in its social, literary, political and other contexts, as shown on pages 58–75. You should write at different levels, moving beyond description to analysis and evaluation. Simply telling the story or describing characters is not as effective as analysing how events or characters embody wider concerns of the play. In *As You Like It*, these wider concerns (also called themes, issues, preoccupations – or, more simply, 'what the play is about') include love (in all its variety), court versus country, appearance and reality, order and disorder, loyalty and service, time, change. In your writing, always give practical examples (quotations, actions) which illustrate the themes you discuss.

How should you answer an examination question or write a coursework essay? The following threefold structure can help you organise your response:

Opening paragraph. Begin with a paragraph identifying just what topic or issue you will focus on. Show that you have understood what the question is about. You probably will have prepared for particular topics. But look closely at the question and identify key words to see what particular aspect it asks you to write about. Adapt your material to answer that question. Examiners do not reward an essay, however well written, if it is not on the question set.

Developing paragraphs. This is the main body of your essay. In it, you develop your argument, point by point, paragraph by paragraph. Use evidence from the play that illuminates the topic or issue, and answers the question set. Each paragraph makes a point of dramatic or thematic significance. Some paragraphs could make points concerned with context or particular critical approaches. The effect of your argument builds up as each paragraph adds to the persuasive quality of your essay. Use brief quotations that support your argument, and show clearly just why they are relevant. Ensure that your essay demonstrates that you are aware that *As You Like It* is a play, a drama intended for performance, and therefore open to a wide variety of interpretations and audience responses.

Concluding paragraph. Your final paragraph pulls together your main conclusions. It does not simply repeat what you have written earlier, but summarises concisely how your essay has successfully answered the question.

Example

The following notes show the 'ingredients' of an answer. In an examination it is usually helpful to prepare similar notes from which you write your essay, paragraph by paragraph. Avoid using 'we' and 'our' (see page 87). Remember that examiners are not impressed by 'name-dropping': use of critics' names. They want you to show your own knowledge and judgement of the play and its contexts, and of how it has been interpreted from different critical perspectives.

> Question: It has been claimed that *As You Like It* is 'a dramatic celebration of love'. Is it?

Opening paragraph

Show that you are aware that the question asks you to give a response to a 'claim' – and claims are always disputable! So include the following points and aim to write a sentence or more on each:

- The play is certainly about love (the word 'love' recurs many times).

- Love appears to be the driving force of the play (within a few minutes of her first appearance Rosalind asks the question 'what think you of falling in love?', and in the forest she plays her intriguing love game with Orlando).
- Hymen, the god of marriage, appears at the end (and the marriage celebrations anticipate 'true delights').
- But 'celebration' implies that love is unambiguously portrayed as joyous, successful and uncomplicated (Shakespeare rarely 'celebrates' – his drama raises questions and shows contradictions).
- *As You Like It* portrays many different kinds of love (and invites audiences to make their own judgements on each).

Developing paragraphs

Now write a paragraph on each of a number of different ways in which the play depicts love. In each paragraph identify the importance (dramatic, thematic, etc.) of the example you discuss. Some of the points you might include are given briefly below. At least one aspect of 'importance' is given in brackets, but there are of course others.

- **Brotherly love:** the reconciliation of Orlando and Oliver (but the play opens with brotherly hate: Orlando is mistreated by Oliver, who plans to have him killed; Duke Frederick has usurped Duke Senior. Even though Orlando saves Oliver from a lion and so converts him to goodness, Duke Frederick is not actually reunited with his brother).
- **Love as friendship and service:** Adam is devoted to Orlando – and Orlando shows compassion towards him in the forest (but Orlando takes Adam's money, and Adam disappears from the play. Amiens sings of man's ingratitude and 'Most friendship is feigning').
- **Self love:** Jaques delights in his pose as cynic and world-weary traveller, promoting his image as malcontent. (He rejects the friendship of his fellow exiles, and opts for loneliness.)
- **Love of power and possessions:** evident in Frederick and Oliver. (In the early part of the play they follow only their own interests. In the forest, Corin's churlish master rejects 'deeds of hospitality' – helping others.)
- **Love as lust:** Touchstone is unequivocal about his sexual desire for Audrey. (There are strong indications that this love affair will not last.)

- **Idealised love:** the pastoral romance tradition portrayal of Silvius and Phebe (but Shakespeare mocks rather than celebrates the doting worship of Silvius for Phebe. He further parodies such sentimental love in Orlando's bad verses).
- **The cruelty of love:** Phebe's scorn for Silvius is typical of the genre of pastoral romance (onstage, Silvius can evoke audience sympathy for his suffering, and Phebe's final acceptance can seem artificial and grudging).
- **Love at first sight:** Shakespeare portrays such instantaneous love in Orlando and Rosalind, Celia and Oliver (but he lampoons it in Phebe's love at first sight for the disguised Rosalind, suggesting not 'celebration' but parody or satire).
- **Sincere love:** Rosalind's love for Orlando, in all its changing moods: she is downcast at Orlando's lateness; her breathless list of questions to Celia, demanding to know who has written poems to her; her delight in hearing Celia talk about Orlando; she relishes the flirting and wordplay in the wooing scene; her sheer exuberance in 'O coz, coz, coz . . .'; she faints at the sight of a handkerchief stained with her lover's blood (all seem to celebrate love).

Concluding paragraph

Write several sentences pulling together your conclusions. You might include the following points which cast doubt on whether the play 'celebrates' love:

- Rosalind's love is clear-sighted and sceptical. She is not fooled by the bad verses that Orlando writes, and she mocks his claim that he will love for ever and a day. There is stark realism in her recognition that 'men have died . . . but not for love'.
- The play appears to end happily in the marriages of the four pairs of lovers. But such an ending is a contrivance of the pastoral romance tradition which Shakespeare has mocked throughout the play.
- *As You Like It* explores a wide variety of viewpoints as characters express and criticise the absurdities and contradictions of love.
- The play is probably more appropriately seen as a searching dramatic exploration of love rather than its celebration.

Writing about character

As the Critical approaches section showed, much critical writing about *As You Like It* traditionally focused on characters, writing about them as if they were living human beings. Today it is not sufficient just to describe their personalities. When you write about characters you will also be expected to show that they are dramatic constructs, part of Shakespeare's stagecraft. They embody the wider concerns of the play, have certain dramatic functions, and are set in a social and political world with particular values and beliefs. They reflect and express issues of significance to Shakespeare's society – and today's.

All that may seem difficult and abstract. But don't feel overwhelmed. Everything you read in this book is written with those principles in mind, and can be a model for your own writing. Of course you should say what a character seems like to you, but you should also write about how Shakespeare makes him or her part of his overall dramatic design. For example, Shakespeare creates dramatic patterns by making characters equivalent or contrasting in their dramatic functions:

- Touchstone and Jaques fulfil similar dramatic functions. Both are ironic commentators on the folly or absurdity of all they see around them, whether court or country, love or music, or language itself.
- Duke Senior and Duke Frederick are, like Orlando and Oliver, contrasting brothers, one 'good', one 'bad'.
- Touchstone and Corin are paired to comment, each in his own way, on the contrasts between court and country.

Another way of thinking of characters is that in Shakespeare's time, playwrights and audiences were less concerned with psychological realism than with character types and their functions. Today, film and television have accustomed audiences to expect the inner life of characters to be revealed. Although Shakespeare's characters do sometimes reveal their inmost thoughts and feelings, especially in soliloquy, his audiences tended to regard them as characters in a developing story, to be understood by how they formed part of that story, and by how far they conformed to certain well-known types and fulfilled certain traditional roles. That is, in *As You Like It*, audiences expected and recognised stock figures of pastoral romance and traditional drama:

- Adam is the 'good old man' who represents an older world of loyal and faithful service.
- Orlando is the high-born young lover who finally wins his love after many trials and ordeals.
- Silvius is the lovelorn faithful shepherd who suffers the pains of unrequited love. Phebe is the disdainful shepherdess, the cruel mistress of pastoral literature, whose beautiful face conceals a hard heart. Speaking in elegant, polished verse, they are traditional figures of the court in the country: courtiers who dress up as shepherdesses and shepherds and create an idealised rural idyll without dirt or labour. Celia in disguise as Aliena can also be seen in this way. But Audrey the goatherd is Shakespeare's invention. She is simple and down-to-earth: a 'real' shepherdess, uneducated and unaware of court manners.
- The melancholy Jaques would today probably be called neurotic or unbalanced. He is the malcontent (see page 72), a familiar role in Elizabethan times, both onstage and in real life. Such characters were expected to be sardonic observers who comment cynically on everything and everybody around them. Their jaundiced, pessimistic view of the world makes them see only foolishness, absurdities and ingratitude.
- Touchstone, 'the motley-minded gentleman', is the court jester who joins Rosalind and Celia in their flight to the Forest of Arden. As a licensed fool his role in court (and onstage) was to comment on what he saw around him, exposing folly and dishonesty. His name signifies his dramatic function. A touchstone was used to find out if a metal was true gold or silver. In the same way, Touchstone tests the genuineness of characters with his sceptical comments. Touchstone is as out of place in the country as Jaques, and he shares some of Jaques' qualities. His role is that of mocking observer, showing up the sham honour and courtesy of the court, and ridiculing love, melancholy and the country.

But there is also a danger in writing about the functions of characters or the character types they represent. Touchstone, for example, is much more than the traditional clown or fool. Actors can create him as a believable human being who obviously loves language, delighting in stories, puns and jokes, sexual *double entendres* and false logic. To reduce a character to a mere plot device is just as inappropriate as treating him or her as a real person. Shakespeare gives even minor characters the opportunity to make a significant impression on the audience as a recognisable human being. For example, both Charles the wrestler and Le Beau might be seen as merely functional characters, briefly brought on to perform a needed dramatic task, then to disappear for ever. But Shakespeare gives each a distinctive voice and occasional turn of phrase that can engage audience sympathy.

When you write about characters in *As You Like It* you should therefore try to achieve a balance between analysing their personality, identifying the dilemmas they face, and placing them in their social, critical and dramatic contexts. That style of writing is found all through this Guide, and that, together with the following brief discussions of three characters (and a surprising fourth), can help your own written responses.

Rosalind

Rosalind is one of the longest parts in all Shakespeare, having more lines than Macbeth or Prospero. She appears first as a typical court lady, enjoying witty wordplay with her cousin Celia. In her early scenes she seems to accept a subordinate role to Celia (it is Celia's suggestion that they leave the court and go to Arden). But as the play moves to the forest, and in her disguise as Ganymede, Rosalind takes the initiative more and more. She controls the action, manipulating other characters and exercising her strong sense of humour as she alternately mocks and celebrates love.

As Rosalind's behaviour changes, so too does her language. She abandons the flowery style of the court in favour of direct and frank analyses of love. She gives full expression to her feelings: 'O coz, coz, coz, my pretty little coz, that thou didst know how many fathom deep I am in love!'

In the forest, disguised as Ganymede, Rosalind woos and tests Orlando, with whom she is head over heels in love. Even in her disguise she retains her femininity, keeping Orlando at a distance as he suggests a kiss: 'Nay, you were better speak first'. She uses her disguise to express her true feelings: 'Come, woo me, woo me; for now I am in a holiday humour and like enough to consent.' And consent she does, tricking Orlando into marrying her, putting the words of the wedding ceremony into his mouth ('"I take thee, Rosalind, for wife"'), and joyously replying 'I do take thee, Orlando, for my husband.'

Rosalind's mood swings violently as she experiences the conflicting emotions that love brings. But for all her rapture, she is clear-eyed about the nature of love: 'men have died from time to time – and worms have eaten them – but not for love.' That sceptical attitude does not prevent her feelings getting the better of her: she faints at the sight of Orlando's blood-stained napkin. Rosalind finally becomes a kind of mistress of ceremonies, arranging the multiple marriages of the final scene. In the Epilogue, Shakespeare reveals yet another aspect of Rosalind's beguiling changeability when he allows his boy actor to acknowledge the cross-dressing role: 'If I were a woman'.

Celia

Celia is daughter of the wicked Duke Frederick, and cousin and best friend of Rosalind. She stands up to her angry father, and proposes the plan of escape to Arden. Shakespeare complicates her character as the play progresses. She seems to becomes more reserved, taking a subordinate role to Rosalind and having less and less to say. She is silent in Act 5. There are strong hints that Celia is genuinely critical of Rosalind in the wooing episode. One interpretation suggests that she becomes increasingly separated from Rosalind, aware that she is losing her best friend.

Orlando

Orlando, like Rosalind, is wrongly treated by a close relative who hates him only for his goodness. His eldest brother denies him education and money, and plans to murder him. After defeating Charles the wrestler, Orlando flees to the Forest of Arden with Adam, his old servant. In the forest he takes on the role of a foolish courtly lover, writing bad verses to his beloved Rosalind, and hanging them on trees. But Rosalind, in disguise as Ganymede, persuades him to woo her, and he discovers true love. Towards the end of the play he is wounded as he saves his wicked brother Oliver from a hungry lion. Orlando's brave action and forgiveness converts his brother to goodness. As the pastoral romance tradition ordains for such young heroes, Orlando achieves wealth, status and happiness: he ends the play heir to Duke Senior and about to marry Rosalind.

The Forest of Arden

It may seem strange to think of the forest as a character. But it plays a vital part in the play, and in many ways typifies the world of pastoral romance. It is a place of escape to the illusion of perpetual holiday and freedom; a place where time stands still ('there's no clock in the forest.'). This contented never-never land of make-believe exists under many names: Utopia, the Big Rock Candy Mountain, Fairyland, Xanadu, Arcadia, the Land of Cockaigne, the Golden Age, Shangri-La, Camelot, New Atlantis, Blue-remembered Hills, Dreamland. It is the biblical Garden of Eden in the days before the Fall.

Shakespeare created similar remote worlds in other plays: Illyria in *Twelfth Night*, the wood near Athens in *A Midsummer Night's Dream*, Belmont in *The Merchant of Venice*, Ephesus in *The Comedy of Errors*. These are festive worlds of romance, full of magical possibilities, where anything can happen. In these exotic locations of Shakespeare's comedies, disguises are adopted, all kinds of confusions, errors and mistakes occur, but the end result is marriage and happiness. All are places where dreams come true.

The myth of the Forest of Arden sees it as a place of perpetual springtime or summer. It is an enchanted, innocent world where happiness is truly possible, where community, brotherhood, and welcoming hospitality are found. It fosters regeneration and reconciliation as characters are changed by their experience, discovering truths about themselves and others. As Charles the wrestler says, Arden is like the 'golden world' of Robin Hood and his Merry Men.

Arden is a refuge from the hypocrisy, deceit and ambition of the court. It is a place of harmony, free from the anger of fathers and brothers, from envy and malice, or the false friendship of flattering courtiers. In modern times many attempts have been made to find similar places of escape and freedom from the realities of everyday life: hippy communes and organic communities.

But, as all the idealistic descriptions above suggest, the Forest of Arden is a fictitious place, a state of mind. It is not the countryside near Stratford-upon-Avon, or the Ardennes region of eastern France. Rather, it is a world which exists in the imagination for a few hours onstage as the play is performed. And Shakespeare's sceptical dramatisation of pastoral romance ensures that the Forest of Arden is not a utopia. In *As You Like It*, Arden has its own perils: harsh winds, cold, low wages, hard masters, dangerous creatures, weariness, hunting and death, hunger and exhaustion. The critic Jan Kott called it 'bitter Arcadia', and characters in the play refer to it as 'a desert'. As the theatre director David Jones remarks:

> Shakespeare is not interested in a comforting pastoral dream. From the dark corridors of the Duke's palace, the forest has all the inviting warmth of the escape world of the Golden Age. But those who make the journey find 'a desert inaccessible', where the wind bites shrewdly, and food is only to be had by hunting. Expecting a womb, they are faced with a challenge. The forest only helps those who help themselves.

A note on examiners

Examiners do not try to trap you or trick you. They set questions and select passages for comment intended to help you write your own informed personal response to the play. They expect your answer to display a sound knowledge and understanding of the play, and to be well structured. They want you to develop an argument, using evidence from the text to support your interpretations and judgements. Examiners know there is never one 'right answer' to a question, but always opportunities to explore different approaches and interpretations. As such, they welcome answers which directly address the question set, and which demonstrate originality, insight and awareness of complexity. Above all, they reward responses which show your perception that *As You Like It* is a play for performance, and that you can identify how Shakespeare achieves his dramatic effects.

And what about critics? Examiners want you to show you are aware of different critical approaches to the play. But they do not expect you simply to drop critics' names into your essay, or to remember quotations from critics. Rather, they want you to show that you can interpret the play from different critical perspectives, and that you know that any critical approach provides only a partial view of *As You Like It*. Often, that need only be just a section of your essay. Examiners are always interested in your view of the play. They expect your writing to show how you have come to that view from thinking critically about the play, reading it, seeing it performed, reading about it, and perhaps from acting some of it yourself – even if that acting is in your imagination!

Resources

Books

C L Barber, *Shakespeare's Festive Comedy*, Princeton University Press, 1959
An important critical study that explores how the social form of Elizabethan holidays contributed to the dramatic form of Shakespeare's comedies. The chapter on *As You Like It* sees Arden as a place of liberty where release from convention leads to understanding.

Harold Bloom, *Shakespeare: The Invention of the Human*, Fourth Estate, 1999
Although the book is censured by most modern critics, Bloom's chapter on *As You Like It* is a thought-provoking example of detailed character study.

John Russell Brown (ed.), *Shakespeare: Much Ado About Nothing and As You Like It: A Casebook*, Macmillan, 1979
Contains a valuable collection of critical writing on comedy and the play from 1623–1977, including the essays by Gardner, Palmer and Latham noted in this booklist.

Malcolm Evans, *Signifying Nothing: Truth's True Contents in Shakespeare's Text*, Harvester, 1986
A postmodern reading which challenges traditional liberal humanist criticism of Shakespeare.

Helen Gardner, 'Let the Forest Judge', in John Russell Brown (ed.), *Shakespeare: Much Ado About Nothing and As You Like It: A Casebook*, Macmillan, 1979
An important essay which argues that the play is centrally concerned with the discovery of truth by feigning, and the use of debate to separate wisdom from folly.

Penny Gay, *William Shakespeare: As You Like It*, Northcote House and British Council, 1999
A mainly feminist reading which identifies how the play raises important issues of sexuality, gender and power, and how those issues may have been made evident on the stage space of Shakespeare's Globe.

Penny Gay, *As She Likes It: Shakespeare's Unruly Women*, Routledge, 1994
Examines how gender politics have affected performances of the comedies. The chapter 'Who's Who in the Greenwood' analyses performances of *As You Like It* at the Shakespeare Memorial Theatre, Stratford-upon-Avon, 1952–1990.

Harley Granville-Barker, *Prefaces to Shakespeare: Love's Labour's Lost, As You Like It, The Merchant of Venice*, Batsford, 1982
A highly influential reading by a theatre practitioner. Essential for students of

stagecraft. Granville-Barker, himself a playwright and director, gives prescriptive advice on staging and characterisation.

Russell Jackson and Robert Smallwood (eds.), *Players of Shakespeare 2 and 3*, Cambridge University Press, 1988 and 1993
Volume 2 contains essays by actors Alan Rickman (on Jaques), Fiona Shaw and Juliet Stevenson (on Celia and Rosalind). Volume 3 contains an essay by Sophie Thompson on Rosalind and Celia.

Frank Kermode, *Shakespeare's Language*, Allen Lane, Penguin, 2000
A detailed examination of how Shakespeare's language changed over the course of his playwriting career. Contains only a brief section on *As You Like It*, but the discussion of other plays can also illuminate understanding of Shakespeare's use of language.

Jan Kott, *Shakespeare our Contemporary*, Methuen, 1965
An influential political reading of Shakespeare's plays. The chapter 'Shakespeare's bitter Arcadia' sees both the court and Arden as equally ruthless and egoistic.

Agnes Latham, 'Satirists, Fools and Clowns', in John Russell Brown (ed.), *Shakespeare: Much Ado About Nothing and As You Like It: A Casebook*, Macmillan, 1979
Identifies Jaques as a type of the contemplative 'melancholy man' of Elizabethan England. Argues that Jaques enjoys his melancholy and does not possess the personal grudges of the traditional malcontent.

Amelia Marriette, 'Urban Dystopias: Re-approaching Christine Edzard's *As You Like It*', in Mark Thornton Burnett and Ramona Wray (eds.), *Shakespeare, Film, Fin de Siècle*, Macmillan, 2000
A postmodern justification of Edzard's film, defending it against criticism of the incongruity of the modern urban setting of the film with the play's language and concerns. Argues the film is a successful postmodern experiment.

Louis Montrose '"The Place of a Brother" in *As You Like It*: Social Process and Comic Form', in Ivo Kamps (ed.), *Materialist Shakespeare*, Verso, 1995
Investigates patriarchy through discussing father–son relationships and brother–brother rivalry. Sees Orlando as a dispossessed younger son commonly found in Elizabethan society.

D J Palmer, '*As You Like It* and the Idea of Play', in John Russell Brown (ed.), *Shakespeare: Much Ado About Nothing and As You Like It: A Casebook*, Macmillan, 1979
A very readable essay that uses 'play' as its concept through which to analyse *As You Like It*.

Peter Reynolds, *As You Like It: A Dramatic Commentary*, Penguin, 1988
Very helpful on the theatrical possibilities of the play. Imagines it staged by three directors who approach *As You Like It* from different standpoints: romance, politics and feminism.

Caroline Spurgeon, *Shakespeare's Imagery and What it Tells Us*, Cambridge University Press, 1935
The first major study of imagery in the plays. Although much criticised today, Spurgeon's identification of image-clusters as a dominant feature of the plays has influenced later studies.

Brian Vickers, *The Artistry of Shakespeare's Prose*, Methuen, 1968
A clear analysis of the language devices Shakespeare uses in his prose. The discussion of *As You Like It* is extremely valuable in its detailed consideration of speeches and dialogue.

Films

A film of *As You Like It*, directed by Yakov Fried, was made in the former USSR in 1955, but is no longer available. A half-hour animated version, adapted by Leon Garfield, is available in the Animated Tales series. The two versions that can usually be obtained on video are:

As You Like It (1979) directed by Basil Coleman.
Made for the BBC/Time Life series, this television version uses Elizabethan–Jacobean costumes and settings.

As You Like It (1996) directed by Christine Edzard.
A modern setting which transforms the court into a corporate business and the forest into an urban wasteland.

Audio books

Four major versions are easily available, in the series by Naxos, Arkangel, HarperCollins and BBC Radio Collection.

As You Like It on the Web

If you type '*As You Like It* Shakespeare' into your search engine, it may find over 50,000 items. Because websites are of wildly varying quality, and rapidly disappear or are created, no recommendation can safely be made. But if you have time to browse, you may find much of interest.